Public Opinion, the First Ladyship, and Hillary Rodham Clinton

PUBLIC OPINION, THE FIRST LADYSHIP, AND HILLARY RODHAM CLINTON

Revised Edition

Barbara Burrell

Routledge
New York & London / 2001

Published in 2001 by
Routledge
29 West 35th Street
New York, NY 10001

Routledge is an imprint of the Taylor & Francis Group

10 9 8 7 6 5 4 3 2 1

Cataloging-in-Publication information is available from
the Library of Congress

ISBN 0-8153-3599-7

For Diane Blair

Contents

Series Editor's Foreword

The goal of the series Women and Politics in Democratic States is to publish original research examining women's participation and how women's politics affect the political life of democratic states. The twentieth century is marked by a gradual, if erratic, inclusion of women as citizens in democracies. In the early years, changes involved legal reforms, removing explicit restrictions on women's rights as citizens to vote and run for office and organizational changes in political parties to include women and their policy concerns. Along with these change were demands—answered with a wide range of policies in most states—that democracies serve the needs of women as workers and mothers. in the last part of the century, women's movements have wanted more than legal reforms and "women friendly" policies. They have demanded power itself, and their campaigns will not be satisfied with anything less than equality in decision making positions. Finally, regimes in the process of transition to democracy around the world are under international pressures that few of the established democracies have experienced: they must show that opening up political competition and securing civil liberties will not ignore equality for women.

Into this political world, where power meets widespread conflict about gender roles, has come Hillary Rodham Clinton, first lady like no other. With *Public Opinion, the First Ladyship, and Hillary Rodham Clinton,* we launch Garland's series on Women and Politics in Democratic States. As readers will discover, Barbara Burrell has identified the major issues of gender and American democratic politics raised by the public life of a unique woman in a unique political role and showcased the profound ambivalence in public opinion produced by a public woman in a private role. It is

ix

remarkable that most of the century's symbolic residue from gender conflicts is embodied in this first lady. Other political wives around the world are inevitably measured against her career, as she has struggled to solve the "problem of the First Ladyship" delineated in this work. Burrell documents not only Clinton's career in this job but also how both images of political wives and the White House are forever marked by the Hillary phenomenon.

Dorothy McBride Stetson

Chapter 1

Introduction

Perhaps it was inevitable that all of the debates, controversies, and conflicts that emanated from the contemporary women's rights movement about women's roles in society would eventually touch one of the most prominent, distinctive, potentially influential, and yet most traditional positions women have occupied in the United States—that of first lady. This occurred in 1992, as Hillary Rodham Clinton traversed the campaign trail on behalf of her husband's quest for the presidency of the United States. She engendered a national discussion, to put it mildly, about the power and influence of women, wives in particular, in the political life of the nation. She sparked the public to think about and struggle with gender politics and the relationship between private life and public life.

Now, after nearly completing her tenure as first lady, Hillary Rodham Clinton continues to be a contradictory symbol. To conservatives she has represented what is "wrong" with America both in terms of the substantive national policies she has advocated and the role she plays as a woman. Liberals and especially feminists try to grapple with the idea of a woman in an unelected and unappointed position wielding political power as a senior advisor to the president. She has twisted all of the clear dividing lines between what political philosophers have considered the private domain, that is, wife, mother, and homemaker, and the public realm of power and influence in the civic life of a community. Of course, Hillary Rodham Clinton had not been primarily a homemaker prior to entering the White House; she had been a prominent professional outside of the home. She represented a new generation of American women who had come into their own.

However, she did not come by her position in the White House because of her professional credentials, but because of her relationship to a man. That is an old-fashioned way of exercising influence in contrast to the women who made headlines as candidates for public office in 1992, during the so-called Year of the Woman in U.S. Politics.

A review of editorials and journalistic analyses during the election of 1992 puts the challenge Hillary Clinton presented to the American public in stark relief. For example, very early she became "a national Roscharch test on which Americans [could] project their views of gender and equality. . . ." For some, she's an inspiring mother-attorney. Others see in her the "overbearing yuppie wife from hell," according to *U.S. News and World Report* (Cooper 1992). Thus one ideological battle was framed as a clash between the professional and the homemaker roles of women. Hillary was characterized as "a new breed of political wife, representing a new generation of working women. To many she is a role model, an inspiration. In other quarters . . . [she] is seen as a brash, overbearing career woman one step away from being a liability. Her outspokenness has made many uncomfortable, even angry" (Hall 1992). This clash was alluded to repeatedly in political commentary during the 1992 campaign.

A second and very much related focus in the debate surrounding Hillary Rodham Clinton centered on the notion of "first lady" and what a person in that position should be like. There was a resistance and a questioning of "the idea of a first lady openly engaged in the affairs of state. . . . The public is still skittish about the idea of a first lady who is more involved in substance than ceremony" (Dowd 1992). Some voters, "particularly older women, are uneasy with the notion that Hillary is ambitious—not just for her husband, but for herself" (Clift 1992), although an analysis of poll data does not necessarily bear out this contention as we will see later. Putting these two fault lines together in the political debate surrounding Hillary Rodham Clinton, that is, women as politicians and wives as influential policy advisors captures the problem for Americans throughout Hillary Rodham Clinton's tenure as first lady.

The debate surrounding Hillary Rodham Clinton touches the core of the challenge the women's movement has presented to our society. As historian Carl Anthony has described it, the "whole first lady issue [is] a lightning rod for something that goes far deeper. And that is the hypocrisy we still have about the status of women. It is a jealousy" (as quoted in Morrison, 1992). Criticism of Hillary Clinton illuminated "society's ambivalence toward changing roles. . . . Men may be projecting on to Mrs. Clinton their hostility toward feminism, while women, overwhelmed by their multiple responsibilities, may be projecting their frustrations" (Pogrebin 1992). But at the same time, many had a strong positive reaction to her; her defenders and champions have also been vocal. As Patricia Ryden put it: "The role of the first lady can be seen as a microcosm of the constraints and contradictory expectations faced by public women due to the tradition of a gender-based public/private dichotomy."

Why do we even have a first lady? Part of the answer lies in the dual leadership role that the president fulfills. The president is both the head of the government, performing executive and legislative duties, and the head of state, presiding over ceremonial functions for the nation and representing the United States in the world. Most other democracies separate these two functions, some with a prime minister and a president. "The American president, charged with both tasks, frequently resorted to sending substitutes on ceremonial and other occasions when a mere physical presence was required. Members of the president's household made excellent surrogates. They signaled the president's approval and also his continued control of government" (Kellerman 1981, 26). Thus, the spouse can serve as a substitute for the head of state for ceremonial functions, and the family becomes a prominent symbol in national life, a sort of royal family. Because we do not have royalty, the "first family" becomes the focus of attention for the media who link them to the public. Thus, the role of hostess has always been of prime concern to presidential spouses (although some in the 19th century did not perform this "duty" for a variety of reasons).

The position of first lady in contemporary times has the potential of becoming an important part of the office of the president beyond the role of assisting with ceremonial head of state duties. Legally she is now considered to be a "de facto" governmental official. (See Chapter 5.) Certainly Hillary Rodham Clinton has had this larger vision of the first ladyship in mind. Because the office of first lady could be transformed into an institutionalized policy making center, a systematic analysis of the people's beliefs about that office and the actions of the person in it is an important part of the study of the contemporary presidency and a significant illustration of how gender affects politics in the United States. The central research focus of this study is the limits and opportunities of the presidential spouse being an overt policy advisor in the White House Office, questions surrounding that possibility, and its linkage to liberal democratic theory which emphasizes the autonomy of the individual. This study integrates this philosophical perspective on individual autonomy and the first ladyship with an analysis of public opinion regarding her role and activities.

First ladies have always been able to exercise private influence if they so desired. Some first ladies historically have been publicly influential, starting with the second first lady, Abigail Adams. But moving toward the more formal notion of a role in policy making is a different step. The role of would-be first ladies as more than cheerleaders for their spouses on the campaign trail did not begin with the 1992 election. In 1987, the Polk County Iowa Democratic Party sponsored a forum with the wives of six of the announced Democratic contenders for the presidency. Each of the wives spoke about the issues that she would pursue in the White House and her vision of the role of first lady. Such a gathering implied that voters should look beyond the man running for the office and examine the ideas of their spouses. It suggested an enlarged role and a policy prominence for future first ladies. Interestingly, however, at the end of her history of first ladies, Betty Caroli concluded in 1987 that the job of first lady might actually decrease in the future. She thought that as wives came to pursue their own professional careers, they would be less likely to drop them if their husband won the presidency (1987, 330). But rather than a contraction of the role, what we are being exposed to with Hillary Clinton in the White House has been an attempt to expand that position into one of a real political partner and at least a quasi member of the government.

In the past two decades scholarship on first ladies has been transformed from a main emphasis on social history to include political science perspectives and broadened theoretical approaches. Numerous studies have provided an historical overview of the presidential spouse's role as first lady and a number of biographical sketches have been written. College courses on the first lady have been offered, symposia have brought together former First Ladies to discuss their legacy, and scholarly panels have been held to measure the significance of presidential wives, such as the 1984 conference titled "Modern First Ladies: Private Lives and Public Duties" held at the Gerald R. Ford Presidential Library, and George Washington University's continuing education series, "The President's Spouse," carried on C-SPAN in the fall of 1994. Historian Lewis Gould has edited a symposium on "Modern First Ladies and the Presidency" in *Presidential Studies Quarterly* (1990). Hillary Rodham Clinton's tenure in the White House has produced a number of articles focusing on media relations and the first lady such as the *Political Communication* symposium "Hillary Rodham Clinton's Image: Content, Control, and Cultural Politics" (April-June 1997).

Two historians of the first lady well articulate her significance to studies of American politics. According to Betty Boyd Caroli, "First Ladies have reflected the status of American women of their time while helping to shape expectations of what women can properly do. They extend our understanding of how women participated in government in ways other than simply voting and holding office" (1987, xxi). Edith Mayo and Denise Meringolo state, "The experience of first ladies bears witness to the ways in which the personal and the political often converge in women's lives. This new angle of vision on first ladies, based on recent scholarship in women's history, places first ladies in the context of the American presidency and the history of women in America and demonstrates their importance in expanding public roles of women" (1994, 7). Further, Gould has noted that, "By the early 1990s the outlines of a distinct research area devoted to First Ladies had emerged where history, political science, and women's studies intersected" (1996, xiii). Scholars have begun to recognize presidential spouses as forces in executive branch administration, policy, and politics.

OUTLINE OF THE BOOK

Hillary Rodham Clinton has challenged the political system. The media, of course, have made much of this challenge to the traditional role of first ladies in both political reporting and in commentaries. (So, too, Clinton political opponents have made an issue of Hillary Rodham Clinton in this role.) The media have also sought to gauge the response of the public to her in this role and thus, have commissioned public opinion polls to ascertain the reaction of the public. These polls are important. They tell us (with all of the caveats of polling methodology) how the people have been affected by this phenomenon. They allow us to explore thinking about the interaction between the public and private in at least one aspect of gender politics. This work as a second edition of *Public Opinion, the First Ladyship, and Hillary Rodham Clinton* expands on the central concern of the first edition. The focus of the first edition was on the first two years of the Clinton presidency, a time during which Hillary Rodham Clinton assumed the most formal role of any first lady in the presidential advisory system. This edition allows us to extend our focus to examine her legacy as first lady with the insights gained from her first six years in the White House. The focus remains on the people's reactions to her and her activities, but this edition also explores her involvement in the presidency more broadly.

This book takes advantage of the many and varied public opinion polls which have measured the people's reaction to Hillary Rodham Clinton and her activities to reflect on public acceptance or disapproval of this changing role for women. The chapters that follow tell the story of public response to Hillary Rodham Clinton as first lady through a description and analysis of public opinion as measured in national and state surveys during the Clinton administration. Hillary Rodham Clinton has been the focus of polls from the early days of the 1992 campaign season. Never before has the public been asked so consistently what they think about a presidential candidate's spouse and a first lady. Not only have people's general responses to her as first lady been surveyed, but how she is viewed by the public in a great variety of domains also has been explored—as policy advisor to the president and head of the Health Care Task Force, as an influential presence in the White House, her personal qualities and characteristics, her own future in politics, and her involvement in the Whitewater real estate deal while serving as first lady of Arkansas. I examine what these polls tell us about Hillary Rodham Clinton's relationship with the people. Most importantly I ask what are the systemic implications of the public's response to this person in this position for how Americans think about women in political leadership roles.

Chapter 2 does four things. It explores the way in which the first ladyship is problematic in the presidential domain. It lays out the theoretical consideration of the relationship between the private sphere and the public sphere as it impinges on the opportunities for and limits on a presidential spouse to fulfill the liberal democratic idea of individualism. It discusses the idea of gender roles and how our perceptions of those roles affect the first ladyship. It then places Hillary Rodham Clinton's claim to political influence in an historical context by considering the political influence of her predecessors.

Chapter 3 begins a more central concentration on the people's reaction to Hillary Clinton focusing on the campaign for the White House in 1992. When she hit the campaign trail in 1992 Hillary stimulated a new research interest on the part of public opinion pollsters—surveying about presidential wives. She was a prominent and controversial figure in the 1992 campaign. Chapter 3 discusses the roles she played in that election. It examines media coverage of her campaign activities and image, considers the nature of the political opposition to her, and analyzes public opinion data to learn how the people reacted to her on the campaign trail and determine the basis of group support and opposition to her. The people's response to her and the discussion and debate her activities sparked about private and public roles were distinctive phenomena of that campaign and contribute to our understanding of the complexities of women achieving political equality.

We should expect a greater polarization in the people's response to Hillary Rodham Clinton than for most former contemporary first ladies because of the image she (and the future president) developed during the campaign for the White House. We should expect a greater intensity of feeling both positive and negative given the national discourse of her role in her husband's campaign and administration. Perhaps she has elicited distinctive responses from men and women, with women among her strongest supporters and men more challenged by her strength, because of the way in which she was using the role of wife in the public sphere.

Chapter 4 chronicles Hillary Clinton's favorability and job approval ratings throughout the Clinton administration (1993–1999). It particularly examines the public's response to her efforts to transform the first ladyship into a more public advisory and policy-making position. Actions and reactions throughout the two terms of the Clinton presidency on the part of both the first lady and the public are analyzed. Multivariate analyses of group support and opposition to her over time are incorporated into these analyses testing hypotheses regarding her favorability ratings. These findings are embedded in a theoretical discussion of the role of first lady. Her level of popularity is also placed in historical context.

Chapter 5 explores the response of the people to the first lady as an overt policy advisor and their views of her influence. I consider both personal responses to Hillary Rodham Clinton in that role and tease out more systemic reactions to that position regarding women in politics. This chapter focuses on the first lady taking on a policy-making or advisory role in the administration. It considers the historical development of the Office of First Lady and her governmental status. It examines public opinion data regarding Hillary's efforts as a policy advisor and head of the Health Care Reform Task Force, and it contains an analysis of how she responded to the backlash over the failed health care reform effort and the continued Whitewater legal problems and continued to influence public policy in more traditionally accepted ways. Data from public opinion survey questions about aspects of the policy-making role of the first lady focus our attention on the central concerns of this work: philosophical and empirical perspectives on a substantive role for a spouse in a presidential administration.

Chapter 6 examines the role of the first lady as a campaigner. This chapter explores Hillary's role in the 1994 and 1998 mid-term elections and the presidential campaign of 1996. Hillary was one of the most popular Democratic campaigners in 1998 after playing a more focused role in the previous two campaigns when she was feared to be a political liability. Wives have become increasingly active on the campaign trail, taken on more complex roles, and established a strategic importance to their husbands' candidacies. Several scholars have even attempted to quantify their effect. I will review these efforts and expand on them by considering the qualitative aspects of Hillary's campaign efforts. This research also explores the strategic uses of Hillary in the various campaigns and of Elizabeth Dole as a presidential wife in the 1996 campaign. The campaign roles of spouses very much address their relationship to the public and their force in administrations.

A further prominent feature of Hillary Rodham Clinton's first ladyship has been her global diplomatic missions. Chapter 7 presents totally new material; it first chronicles her international travels, with an emphasis on her foreign policy missions regarding women's rights. Hillary Rodham Clinton took over twenty solo journeys abroad as first lady. This chapter then combines an analysis of the nature of the feminism she espoused globally as an individual, an examination of the extent to which she served in a governmental capacity in foreign affairs, and whether this is a new facet of the Office of First Lady. While Hillary made a conscious effort not to negotiate foreign policy as a representative of her husband as Rosalynn Carter had in Latin America, she did represent the government in announcing aid packages in foreign trips. She also publicly supported human rights

issues. These activities were much broader and substantively more important than the traditional goodwill trips of former first ladies. They were
diplomatic missions signifying a new dimension to first lady activism, and
they must be considered if we are to make a comprehensive assessment of
the new governmental status of the first lady.

Chapter 8 concludes this work with a discussion of the philosophical
perspective driving this work. It reflects on the possibilities of the presidential spouse acting as a policy advisor and considers the evidence of public support for that role. It examines the issue of accountability and argues
for a freedom of choice for the presidential spouse to seek achievement as
an individual.

Hillary's tenure as first lady can be divided into three time phases for
purposes of public opinion analyses: the first two years of the first administration (1993–1994) during the time of the Health Care Reform Task
Force; the last two years of the first administration (1995–1996) during
which time she tried to recover her popularity by refocusing her advisory
tasks and performance. She continued to struggle with the Whitewater
scandal during these years. She also became more internationalist in her
activities. The second administration forms a third phase in which she has
carved out a very distinctive first ladyship that has combined an outspoken
advocacy for traditional issues of importance to women and children,
major campaigning for Democratic candidates in the 1998 election, and an
effort to stand up for the president (and the presidency) after Bill Clinton's
scandalous behavior which, perhaps more than anything, insulted her. The
latter set of events highlighted her role as wife as opposed to independent
actor, which had been her aim throughout the Clinton presidency up to
that time. Her image during this phase provides a challenging piece of
analysis in reflecting on the first lady and liberal feminism.

Hillary Rodham Clinton has come full circle in terms of her popularity:
from being seen as a problem in the Clinton campaign in 1992, to achieving a high level of popularity in 1993, as she became a formal policy advisor in the Clinton administration, to the failure of health care reform in
1994, to emerging at the end of 1998 as one of the most popular
Democrats and a widely admired individual (as opposed to her husband
who had become only the second president to be called to an impeachment
trial). Hillary's activities as first lady provide substantial material for an
extensive and distinctive analysis of the role of first lady, that in turn provides a lens for us to reflect on the role of women and political power and
consideration of gender in American politics.

Chapter 2

Public and Private Domains, Gender Politics, and Political Wives

T he first ladyship is problematic for the presidential domain if we are to consider individuals in this position in the context of women's rights, and if a person in this position wishes to go beyond its traditional activities to play a more formal role in government. It is problematic because the position is associated with the public/private dichotomy that has structured society, and it is problematic because gender affects how we think about and evaluate that role.

THEORETICAL AND HISTORICAL BACKGROUND

The division of the community into public and private realms is a socially determined construct. The private realm centers on home and family while the public realm is concerned with making rules for the community and the enforcement of those rules. Political philosophers established the public realm as the higher domain and assumed that only certain men should participate in that arena. Society constructed these divisions, confining women to the private realm because it was believed that women were incapable of performing competently in the public sector. Patriarchal societies were established, in which men dominated over women, and women were prohibited from speaking publicly. A central issue for feminists has been this division of the world into private and public domains and implications of this dichotomy for women's equality. They have sought to break women's silence.

The major assumptions of patriarchal society have been that men are naturally stronger, superior to, and more rational than women, who are naturally weaker, inferior in intellect, and unstable emotionally and thus are incapable of political participation. Men are destined to be dominant and act in the political world. They represent the polity. Women stand out-side the polity. "Men by their rational minds, explain and order the world. Women by their nurturant function sustain daily life and the continuity of the species" (Lerner 1993, 4).

Aristotle laid the foundation for this philosophical development. He asserted that woman was "naturally" inferior to man. The highest good was achievable only through involvement in public life, for which woman was constitutionally unfit. She was controlled by emotion, not by reason. According to Aristotle, the female's primary function was reproduction. She was to provide domestic services and to carry out household tasks in order to free men to participate in public life. Silence was her glory in Aristotle's thought.

Families and family life, while clearly inferior to public life, were con-sidered the core of the community and necessary to allow those engaged in public life the freedom to be invloved (Okin 1979). For centuries, women were confined to the private sphere, viewed as inferior creatures. They were never given the tools, particularly education, to allow them to develop a sense of self and to learn to speak for themselves in the polity (Lerner 1993). In western political theory women were primarily considered in ref-erence to domestic relationships, viewed only as wives and mothers. Aristotle's intellectual heirs in the eighteenth and nineteenth centuries even claimed that if women engaged in public speaking and other political activ-ities they would damage their wombs (Jamieson 1988, 69). If they spoke, they would also threaten male dominance (Bardes and Gossett 1990).

In the revolutionary era in America, women were energized by the quest for independence and active in the resistance to British rule. (See, e.g., Evans 1989.) The economic boycott that American leaders used against Great Britain mandated the involvement of women because it "could suc-ceed only if white housewives and their daughters refused to purchase imported goods and simultaneously increased their production of home-spun" (Norton 1980). "Boycotts politicized their daily activities of shop-ping and home manufacture" (Evans 1989: 49). Women wrote patriotic poems and political tracts, signed public petitions, raised money for the cause, and demonstrated (Evans 1989). By the 1780s, women were "read-ing widely in political literature, publishing their own sentiments, engaging in heated debates over public policy, and avidly supporting the war effort in a variety of ways" (Norton 1980).

As a result of the war effort, women struggled to conceive of a more political role for themselves. Sadly, the ideology of the American Revolution offered them no positive role in political life. What did emerge was the idea of the "Republican Mother." ". . . The ideology of Republican womanhood was an effort to bring an older version of the separation of spheres into rough conformity with the new politics that valued autonomy and individualism. Issues of sexual asymmetry dominated public discourse to an unprecedented extent as people tried to define a place for women in postrevolutionary society" (Kerber 1980, 20). "The Republican Mother integrated political values into her domestic life. Dedicated as she was to the nurture of public-spirited male citizens, she guaranteed the steady infusion of virtue into the Republic" (Kerber 1980, 11). In her new private role, woman would not only provide physical sustenance to those engaged in the public life of the community, she would undertake the duty of developing political character in potential leaders and citizens. "The Republican Mother was to encourage in her sons civic interest and participation. She was to educate her children and guide them in the paths of morality and virtue" (Kerber 1980, 283). Thus, women could claim a significant political role, although it was to be played in the home. "The problem of female citizenship was solved by endowing domesticity itself with political meaning" (Evans 1989, 57).

A consensus developed in the years of the early Republic "around the idea that a mother, committed to the service of her family and to the state, might serve a political purpose. . . . This new identity had the advantage of appearing to reconcile politics and domesticity; it justified continued political education and political sensibility [which women were seeking]. But the role remained a severely limited one; it had no collective definition, provided no outlet for women to affect a real political decision" (Kerber 1980, 12). Citizenship was defined in gendered terms. The revolutionaries left intact the law of domestic relations that systematically merged the civic identity of women with that of their husbands. Husbands then controlled both their wives' bodies and their property. Married women had no will of their own (Kerber 1995).

After the American Revolution, women continued to be silenced in the public realm, but they began to challenge that silence. Beginning with the women's rights convention in Seneca Falls, New York, in 1848, women called for a more direct political role for themselves. That role eventually centered on obtaining the vote. Suffragists initially argued that equal justice demanded that women be given the vote. Their position was that "if all men were created equal and had the inalienable right to consent to the laws by which they were governed, women were created equal to men and had the same inalienable right to political liberty. In asserting that natural right applied also to women, the suffragists stressed the ways in which men and women were identical. Their common humanity was the core of the suffragist argument" (Kraditor 1965, 44). In her "Solitude of Self" address before the U.S. Senate Committee on Woman Suffrage on February 20, 1892, Elizabeth Cady Stanton argued that first a woman must be considered as an individual, second as a citizen, third as a woman, and fourth as a mother and wife.

Later suffragists stressed differences rather than similarities between men and women as the basis of their rationale for wanting the franchise. They filled their speeches with suggestions that if women became political participants, private morality would override public immorality (Elshtain 1974). The suffragists in the Age of Progressivism emphasized that if women were given the vote, reforms in government would occur. As food and clothing production, activities once performed almost exclusively in the home, became commercialized, they became the subject of legislation. Governmental regulation expanded. It was in women's interest to see that sound laws were passed and implemented in these areas so that they could be good housekeepers. "As the functions which they had previously performed as isolated individuals at home became social functions, women's claim to political equality changed from a demand for the right to protect themselves as individuals to an assertion of their duty to serve society as women. They assumed that their training as cooks, seamstresses, house cleaners, and mothers qualified them to help in legislation concerned with food inspection, sweatshop sanitation, street-cleaning, and public schools" (Kraditor 1965, 68). Women were qualified for lawmaking because government was now involved in large-scale housekeeping. The suffragists argued for the vote in order to better perform their duties as wives, mothers, and housekeepers. Progressive women reformers expanded the Republican Mother ideal as they "saw their commitment to honest politics, efficient urban sanitation, and pure food and drug laws as an extension of their responsibilities as mothers" (Kerber 1980, 284). For example, Jane Addams speaking to the National American Women's Suffrage Association in 1906 argued that:

> City housekeeping has failed partly because women, the traditional housekeepers, have not been consulted as to its multiform activities. The men have been carelessly indifferent to much of this civic housekeeping, as they have always been indifferent to the details of the household. The very multifariousness and complexity of a city government demand the help of minds accustomed to detail and variety of work, to a sense of obligation for the health and welfare of young children and to a responsibility for the cleanliness and comfort of other people. Because all these things have traditionally been in the hands of women, if they take no part in them now they are not only missing the education which the natural participation in civic life would bring to them but they are losing what they have always had (Buhle and Buhle 1978, 371).

Suffragists expressed little interest toward women's political involvement beyond obtaining the vote. They wished to use the vote to bring about public policy change but presumably did not see women as making these changes themselves as political leaders in public office.[1] They did not expect enfranchisement to lead to a radical redefinition of gender roles (Sims 1995). "Women would use the vote to change society, but the vote would not change women" (Elshtain 1982).

The second women's movement in the 1960s redefined women's place in politics. Now women began to organize to achieve an equal role in government for themselves. Activists felt that women should not only participate in the election of political leaders, they should become leaders themselves. Contemporary feminists also sought to eliminate the rigid line between what was public and what was private. They argued that "public and private could not be dealt with as separate worlds, as if one exists in a rhythm independent of the other . . . relations inside family and household are knocked into appropriate shape by a battery of public policies" (Phillips 1991).

The National Organization for Women (NOW), the foremost women's rights organization in the United States in the contemporary era, was founded in 1966 with a call for equal participation and treatment of women in employment, education, and government. Its founding statement had the aim "To take action to bring women into full participation in the mainstream of American society *now,* exercising all the privileges and responsibilities thereof in truly equal partnership with men." Task forces were established to address issues of employment, education, religion, the family, the mass media, politics, and poverty. NOW has developed national, state and local organizational bases.

Later, women in Congress would organize their own caucus to promote issues of special concern to women.[2] A prime issue for the caucus has been the Economic Equity Act, which is a compendium of proposed bills dealing with pensions and retirements, displaced homemakers, nondiscrimination in insurance, care of children and other dependents, and child support enforcement. Many of its provisions have been aimed at homemakers and women on the bottom of the economic ladder (Burrell 1994; Gertzog 1995; Thompson 1999).

Other organizations have formed with the primary aim of electing more women to public office, but women have not been fully integrated into political life because of the constraints of their private lives, particularly their roles as wives, mothers, and homemakers. These constraints are both psychological and substantive. As Sapiro (1983) has found, attitudes toward equality and feelings of political efficacy among women are related to marriage, motherhood, and employment. Only when women can earn as much as men and have the same access to employment opportunities, when they are not considered to be the primary child care givers and men are integrated into the world of the home, will women be able to achieve an integration into political life. Each aspect of women's private roles has political significance and consequences that contemporary women's rights' activists have articulated and attempted to make part of the public policy agenda. Jamieson explains this dichotomy as a double bind that women are striving to break out of (1995).

PUBLIC AND PRIVATE DOMAINS AND THE ROLE OF FIRST LADY

The symbol of the first lady in U.S. politics joins in a unique way the two domains of public and private life. This position has the potential to dramatically alter the idea of what is private and what is public in the political realm. The woman who serves as first lady is there because of her relationship to a man, not through her own achievements. She is to represent the expressive, supportive, traditional role of women as wife, mother, and homemaker. The word "first" suggests that she is to be a role model. "Lady," in this context, suggests a "certain kind of appearance, manners, and demeanor with connotations of middle- and upper-class respectability" (Mayo and Meringolo 1994). These expectations set up a conflict for first ladies: as presidents' wives, they are inevitably on the political stage; they take on a public persona, but as "ladies" they are expected to stay out of politics. Unelected and unappointed, the political influence of first ladies is questioned. As women, their participation becomes suspect and controversial. It is these two aspects of the role—accountability and gender—that cause political and social stress.

The position of first lady is full of cultural contradictions. Originally spouses were not publicly involved in electoral campaigns. Politics was outside of women's domain; it was viewed as a corrupt, dirty activity that would sully women. Later, the role of president's spouse evolved into an electoral asset to be used on the campaign trail. For example, Republicans held "Pat Nixon for first lady" week during the 1960 campaign, scheduling women's luncheons and coffees to win votes. On this campaign stage, however, the candidate's spouse was only suppose to urge people to become involved and support her husband, not to talk about public policy herself or express her own views.

As White House hostess, the first lady can not only make people feel welcome but can also make political statements with how and whom she entertained. Many first ladies became quite adept at combining entertainment with advancing their husbands' political goals. The Smithsonian Institute exhibit "First Ladies: Political Roles and Public Images" provides an overview of this activity. Dolley Madison's entertaining, for example, had its political side as well as social. She "showed the skill of a candidate running for office, rarely forgetting a name or making an inappropriate comment" (Caroli 1987, 14). On the other hand, her successor, Elizabeth Monroe, caused a crisis in the cabinet because she refused to perform the hostess role as it was defined in that era. First ladies could also be advocates for public causes but only for issues in particular domains, "appropriate" issues that few would argue against, such as literacy and volunteerism.

Several books examining first ladies' roles in historical context (e.g., Anthony 1990, 1991; Caroli 1987; Gutin 1989; Gould 1996), the creation of the permanent exhibit "First Ladies: Political Roles and Public Images" at the Smithsonian, and numerous seminars and conferences in recent years have called our attention to the *political* history of the first ladies. In this context, Hillary Rodham Clinton becomes the "latest in a long line of politically astute women who have been intimately involved with their husbands' political careers and administrations" (Mayo 1993). Her command and use of the position, however, as we will see, differs not only in degree from that of her predecessors but in its nature. "The fact is that Hillary Clinton has gone well beyond all her modern predecessors in her engagement in her husband's government. She may have the independent spirit of Betty Ford, shrewdness of Lady Bird Johnson, the seriousness of Rosalynn Carter, etcetera, down the line, but she is something different from all of these and more than the sum of their attributes. She is a strong, separate source of power inside the administration with a mandate of authority from the president and an operational base from which to carry it out" (Greenfield 1993).

Throughout the history of the presidency, first ladies have given political advice to their husbands and served as political confidants (some more than others). Abigail Adams, the second first lady, was the first presidential partner (and was severely criticized in the press for it, derisively called "Mrs. President"). Carl Anthony, who has perhaps most extensively examined the political roles of the first ladies creates a picture of early presidential spouses as very active in politics, often quite public about it, and exerting a great deal of influence in Washington (Anthony 1990). They advocated public policy, were instrumental in political appointments, and sometimes served as messagers to and from the president. They were also subject to much criticism because of their public role.

First ladies in the latter half of the nineteenth century, while focusing on the role of hostess, tended to exert private influence over political affairs, serving as advisors to their husbands behind the scenes. For example, Carl Anthony (1991) reports that "[m]any believed that Mrs. [Rutherford B.] Hayes secretly wielded a heavy magic wand over her husband's policies," and that "[i]f [Caroline Harrison's] primary public role was exemplary goodwife, she was privately a political power . . . she knew her husband's stand on issues, and even promoted them by sending out copies of one of his speeches to Republican leaders."

In the early twentieth century, first ladies "began to play more overtly

political roles" (Mayo 1993), and the office of first lady began to be institutionalized when Edith Roosevelt hired a "social secretary" in 1901, the
first salaried government employee to answer to the first lady as boss
(Anthony 1990, 295). Caroli characterizes the tenure of the four first ladies
at the start of the twentieth century as altering "the meaning of the title
they held. What had been unusual before 1900—the contribution of significant work of their own—became common among Presidents' wives" in
the first two decades of the 1900s (Caroli 1987, 152).

THE INFLUENCE OF FIRST LADIES

While some first ladies have been influential in the public realm and acted
as presidential partners, the nature of their influence has varied. What historical precedents might Hillary Rodham Clinton have looked to in support of her activist public role? When historians have characterized first
ladies as being influential, they did not have policy decision-making exclusively in mind. First ladies' influence on presidential politics has been of
four types. One involves directing and promoting a spouse's career, including climbing the political ladder. Helen Taft was a prominent practitioner
of this type of influence. Among other things, she persuaded William Taft
not to accept a Supreme Court appointment as it would preclude his being
available for a presidential nomination. Florence Harding, another first
lady adept at this type of influence, is quoted as saying "I know what's best
for the president, I put him in the White House" (Anthony 1990, 393).
These women's own ambition was advanced through the careers of their
husbands.

   A variant of this type of influence involves the protection of the health
and well-being of one's spouse once he assumes the strenuous position of
chief executive of the land (Caroli 1987). Caroli believes it was this latter
that characterized Edith Wilson's sway over the White House when
Woodrow Wilson lay ill in 1919 and 1920, rather than a desire for command over policy making. According to Caroli, Nancy Reagan's role during her husband's campaigns and presidency could be described in similar
terms: "she saw her job as protecting him from overwork, inadequate staff,
and poor scheduling. . . . This particular view of the role of a president's
wife had very little to do with the kind of work he did, and should not be
confused with the blatantly political roles that other women such as Helen
Taft, Sarah Polk, Abigail Adams, and Rosalynn Carter took in their husbands' administrations" (1987, 150).

   The second type of influence involves concern with and control over the
social hierarchy of life in the Capitol. At times achieving this goal meant
having a say over presidential appointments, thus, indirectly affecting policy. Given that women were not allowed to exercise direct political power,

their only outlet often became petty political intrigues around personalities. First ladies have been accused of having a keen interest in personnel decisions while in the White House, often basing their "judgments on subjective or irrelevant considerations" (Caroli 1987, 132). Mary Todd Lincoln was a prime example. Or note Helen Taft's comment regarding an appointment to her husband's cabinet, "I could not believe you to be serious when you mentioned that man's name. He is perfectly awful and his family are even worse" (Gould 1985). Hillary Rodham Clinton's involvement in the dismissal of the White House travel office staff in 1993 would seem to fall into this domain rather than being a reflection of her transformation of the first ladyship into a public advisory position.

The third type of influence concernes what is good for the president politically with the president's wife serving as political advisor, and the fourth is the first lady's concern with public policy. Abigail Adams set a precedent by being very much engaged in these latter two types of influence. Sarah Polk, an early presidential spouse, was also very much the president's political and policy making partner in the 1840s. She is even said to have remarked that if she went to the White House she would "neither keep house, nor make butter.[3] . . . I always take a deep interest in state and national affairs" (Anthony 1990, 141).

While other first ladies had acted behind the scenes in promoting public policy, Ellen Wilson broke new ground for a more substantial policy making role for first ladies, although she served only a brief tenure in the White House between 1913 and 1914 before she died. She took a prominent leadership position in housing reform in the early months of Woodrow Wilson's presidency, starting an investigation of Washington's slums. Her name was attached to a slum clearance bill that Congress passed at the time of her death. It was the first piece of legislation passed with such direct and public assistance from a president's wife (Caroli 1987, 134).

Eleanor Roosevelt and Rosalynn Carter were even more active, testifying before Congress on behalf of their projects. Eleanor Roosevelt spoke about the concerns of coal miners and the people of the District of Columbia, while Rosalynn Carter testified on mental health concerns. Hillary Rodham Clinton would go one step further by assuming the lead before Congress regarding a major policy proposal of her husband's administration—health care reform. In this endeavor she has broken "the traditional expectation that the first lady stay out of the political realm and not infringe upon the president's sphere" (Ryden 1993, 15).[4]

HILLARY RODHAM CLINTON AND THE ROLE OF FIRST LADY

The nature and complexity of influence across the spectrum of first ladies awaits further analysis especially as an historical link for Hillary Rodham

Clinton's tenure in that position. She follows in a certain tradition while also being a path breaker. Hillary Rodham Clinton's image has been one of a transformer of the position of first lady. She came to the White House representing a new era, the age of the professional woman, the smart woman. She would not exercise influence behind the scenes and then sit gazing adoringly at her husband while he was on stage. As the *Wall Street Journal* characterized her potential in December 1992, she "promises to be something unique: both a major political power center in her own right, and the first modern working mother in the White House" (Frisby 1992). According to *The Economist,* "[T]here has never before been a woman in the White House who had both a successful career and an independent powerbase before she arrived there. . . . She is a genuine trail-blazer" (December 5, 1992: 30). Clinton views herself as a transition figure (Quindlen 1994c). She promised to be an active, public "partner" in policy making. Clinton's philosophy is that the public and private are thoroughly interconnected. She thus violates the traditional separation of the masculine sphere and the feminine, domestic sphere that previously defined the role of first lady (Ryden 1993).

Hillary Rodham Clinton does have historical predecessors for her active public role as suggested above, especially in Rosalynn Carter, who also headed her own commission and sat in on cabinet meetings. (Although banned from legally being the chair of the President's Commission on Mental Health, it was her commission.) Indeed, a 1979 *Newsweek* cover story on Rosalynn as "The President's Partner" reads uncannily like an analysis of Hillary Rodham Clinton's first period in the White House. The first lady is even referred to as Rosalynn *Smith* Carter in the story (emphasis added) (Morgenthau 1979). Perhaps, given changing views on women in society as the feminist movement grew and developed, Rosalynn Carter would have been credited with creating a more acceptable public policy-making role for the first lady had she not been followed by two first ladies who represented an earlier type of presidential spouse (and had Jimmy Carter been re-elected). But Hillary's predecessor for her very public policy-making position is more often said to be Eleanor Roosevelt than Rosalynn Carter. She herself has even stressed Eleanor Roosevelt as a role model.

Historian Doris Kearns Goodwin offered Hillary advice upon entering the White House from the lessons of Eleanor's tenure that will become significant as we explore the public's reaction to Hillary as first lady. According to Goodwin,

> As you stake out your positions, some people will be angry with you. Thirty percent of the country probably thought Eleanor was the worst person ever to exist, a subversive agitator. . . . Although Eleanor engendered controver-

sial feelings in some, at the same time she was an inspiration for others, particularly blacks but also young women, who saw her doing things women had never done before. The advice Eleanor would give you is: Don't worry about your public opinion polls. Know that you're doing a good job when your friends respect you and your enemies are angry. One of the reasons Barbara Bush has had a 90 percent popularity rating is that she hasn't done anything. She may be warm and affectionate, but she won't leave any accomplishments behind. Don't feel constrained by polls, and don't worry about hurting your husband's political standing (1993).

First Ladies Roosevelt and Clinton share similarities in how they shaped the position of first lady even though important differences exist. They both expressed a public commitment to policy concerns using their position as first lady as a forum to call attention to national problems. Both were the subjects of criticism because of their political views. (See Goodwin 1993.) Each has been considered more liberal than their husbands.

Eleanor Roosevelt and Hillary Rodham Clinton have been perceived as role models for women seeking to expand their individualism and autonomy in society. But although Eleanor Roosevelt promoted greater equality and individualism for women, as a product of her time, she stressed a social feminism in keeping with a distinctive role for women in society. She did not view women as equal with men in the world of politics. She supported protective labor legislation for women and opposed the Equal Rights Amendment being promoted by the Women's Party at that time. She did believe that women should be partners with their husbands first and homemakers second and that they should develop their own interests. She supported careers for women and spoke out on the right of wives to work. (See Caroli 1987.) Hillary, having the advantage of growing up in an age of increasing independence and expanding opportunities for girls and women, has stressed a more liberal feminism, seeing women as equal with men in all facets of life. Women's autonomy and independence are to be promoted. Women's roles are not to be particularly distinct from men's roles for liberal feminists.

Eleanor Roosevelt developed a career as a journalist after becoming first lady, although she had initially feared the first ladyship might prevent her from having an autonomous existence. It was important to her to establish herself as a professional. In the opinion of her family, Eleanor Roosevelt wanted and needed a career to justify her own self worth (Beasley 1987, 68). She, in part, achieved a peripatetic role in national politics because of her husband's limited ability to travel. She might have been kept more in the background and been forced into serving as hostess to a greater extent had polio not constrained the president's activities. However great her national influence, Eleanor Roosevelt was never part of FDR's inner circle of advisors, although some have considered her part of his "Kitchen

Cabinet" (Caroli 1987). She acted as a gadfly in the administration and lobbied her husband along with others.

Hillary, on the other hand, had established a professional career prior to entering the White House (that she had to downplay as would-be first lady). She is also part of the president's inner circle of advisors and is considered a force in policy making. She plays a more central role than Eleanor did. However, after the failure of the Health Care Task Force, which she headed, Hillary adopted a style more in keeping with that of Eleanor Roosevelt. She increasingly stressed the role of outside advocate and began a newspaper column that while being policy oriented on occasion also focused on the personal side of the White House. Eleanor had for years written a daily newspaper column called "My Day."

What has made Hillary Rodham Clinton's tenure in the White House a watershed is her representation of a new generation, and the fact that she is seen as a product of the feminist movement. As Goodwin pointed out, "There's such a power base among women now that, if [Hillary] mobilize[d] them, [she would] be stronger than Eleanor ever was" (1993). It is Hillary's relationship to the feminist movement that is crucial and makes the analyses undertaken in this book important. In her challenge to traditional expectations of first ladies, she reconstructs their role through a fusing of the public and private (Ryden 1993).

She comes to her position at a time when women have redefined their roles and taken advantage of the changes in society that have resulted from the contemporary women's movement to expand their opportunities. Women are now the majority of college students, and while a "glass ceiling" still prevents many women from moving to the top in the business world, they are becoming doctors, lawyers, managers, and other professionals in greater numbers. When earlier first ladies acted politically, they were depicted as exceptions or curiosities. They might have been greatly admired, but they were not necessarily viewed as models for women in general.

There is greater significance to Hillary's actions. She has greater potential for altering the separation of private and public spheres in the sense that a private role may become a legitimate basis for public actions. One's role in the private sphere is not oppositional to performing a public role and being involved in making policy decisions for society. There is an intersection of what we think of as private and public. Her activism more generally focuses attention on women as political leaders. This is what is so unnerving to some and so full of potential to others. The ambivalence about women's changing roles in our society has made the idea of an activist Hillary Rodham Clinton in the role of first lady an enigma.

What is distinctive in the role of first lady is the use of the private role as a basis for participation in public policy making. The first lady does not move out of the private realm into the public as do many women who use experience gained as wives, mothers, and homemakers as bases for community activity, which, in turn, is used as credentials for seeking public office. The first lady meshes the private and the public realms, and that merging may be accepted by the public as legitimate and the occupant of that position may be viewed as a political leader (as well as an admired person). Of course, Hillary had been a public and professional person prior to the Clintons' quest for the White House, so to have expected her to serve only as White House hostess would have been unrealistic and naive. To use her own words, "The idea that I would check my brain at the White House door just doesn't make any sense to me" (Reed 1993).

For most of the contemporary feminist era, as more and more women have sought elective office and women's groups have organized to promote more women as lawmakers and chief executives, attempts have been made to neutralize stereotypes of female politicians. Women tried to show that they could compete in a man's world and that the private world was irrelevant. In the 1992 election that strategy changed, most prominently when Patty Murray ran a successful campaign for the U.S. Senate in Washington State as "just a mom in tennis shoes." Her theme emerged from an opponent's put-down of her background. In 1994, however, female candidates for public office became proactive in promoting their private roles as not only a basis from which to launch a political career but as a positive context in which to run for public office. One should vote for them (among other reasons) because they were mothers. They promoted their motherhood with slogans such as "a Mom, not a millionaire" or "a mom with a mortgage." People were supposed to vote for them precisely because they were mothers and had had certain experiences that their opponents had not had. Out of these experiences, they believe, have come perspectives important to bring to the policy-making process. One candidate for the U.S. House of Representatives, Zoe Lofgren, even went so far as to challenge the establishment as to try to put "mother" on the ballot as part of her job description. It was ruled not a legitimate job.[5]

The first lady position still causes concern, however. Reflecting on presidential candidate spouses, Campbell (1993) has noted that "[w]omen candidates ask voters to revise the relationship between women and public power. By contrast, candidates' wives raise the more problematic issue of the relationship between women, *sexuality*, and power. That is, spouses exert their power by virtue of their sexual and marital relationship to the candidates; their influence is indirect and intimate, a subtle intrusion of the private into the public, political sphere" (p. 1). This is most threatening to men who have viewed the home and their homemaker-wives as a refuge from the world of economic and political power. If a woman can exert influence through her private role as spouse without holding a formal position in the public realm, this dramatically challenges relative positions and power structures in society. Johnson and Broder cited a variation on this theme in their analysis of the health care reform process of the Clinton administration. They commented that the appointment of the first lady as head of the Task Force had created problems because "the person who is in charge shouldn't sleep with the president, because if you sleep with the president, nobody is going to tell you the truth . . ." (1996, 101).

The problematic issue is one of gender and position (and implications for power), or what used to be derisively called "petticoat government." It is the particular nature of combining the personal and the political. As one journalist posed the problem "Why does the prospect of Hillary Clinton as attorney general bother some of us more than the reality of John Kennedy's brother?" (Pollit 1993). Unelected advisors are part of any adminsitration. Why is the idea of wives of political figures wielding power on their own so unsettling to Americans, even political liberals? Feminists, too, seemed to be uneasy about Hillary's role as first lady rather than as presidential candidate, at least as intimated by the media. One has to achieve on one's own to be a legitimate actor in the public realm. It is part of the individu-alistic culture of U.S. society.

The feminist movement sees political wives as becoming independent actors, able to pursue their own interests and careers, rather than being constrained to play the supportive spouse and political hostess to further their husbands' careers. Political spouses like Rosalynn Carter and Hillary Rodham Clinton, rather antithetical to the prescription of the movement, have used their relationship with their spouse to achieve influence instead of seeking their own identity. (See Greenfield 1977.)

The idea of first lady in the political process, then, is full of complexity. First and foremost is the issue of gender. It matters that we are talking about *women* in this role for all of the historical and political reasons that have been cited. Gender politics involves the social construction of biolog-ical sex that gives rise to behaviors, roles, and ways of being, knowing, and doing within institutions (Duerst-Lahti and Kelly 1995). Gender is "a set of practices, a performance, something we 'do'" (Duerst-Lahti 1997, 12). Gender politics implies that activities are viewed differently if performed by men or women, and that masculinity and femininity pervade organization-al behaviors. Gender power relations have effectively excluded women from government. Women have been largely absent from images of politi-cal leaders as well as from the set of practices involved with leadership and governance (Duerst-Lahti and Kelly 1995; Kenney 1996). The executive branch has very much been a masculine institution with its chiefs, com-manders, and hierarchies. (See, e.g., Duerst-Lahti 1997.)

A vivid example of the impact of gender politics in considerations of White House governance and the role of the presidential spouse in it, occurred when Hillary Rodham Clinton headed the Health Care Reform Task Force. Her presence as head placed her in a position of power and leadership usually accessible only to men. A contradiction was perceived between the "wifely" role of the first lady and the power of her position as chair of the Task Force. As Guy (1995) pointed out, "By taking the lead in the Clinton administration's health reform effort, Hillary Rodham Clinton transformed the gender power of the post. . . . Hillary and her policy performance consciously and explicitly challenge the dominance and deference pattern evident in masculinity/femininity, husbands/wives, doctors/nurses, leader/followers."

Second, and also very significant, it the fact that we are talking about a private and deeply personal relationship—marriage—that has public implications. Third, we are considering a traditional symbol, first lady, an icon that has developed roles and images with great meaning for the public, that is being transformed. Fourth is the issue of accountability. If the person who serves in this role desires to be a political force, then how does the public hold her accountable for her influence? The first lady has no formal position in the government. She receives no pay. She receives no confirmation from the U.S. Senate for her job. She cannot be fired. (She could be divorced, but that is a private matter.) Other advisors answer only to the president, but they can be dismissed. In the end, the first lady is held indirectly accountable through the job her husband does as president.

The ultimate scholarly concern of this work emerges from my interest in the concept of the first ladyship, its connection to our idea of liberal democracy, its relationship with the women's rights movement and gender roles in our society, and its place in the presidency. Liberal democratic ideas impinge on the role of first lady in a number of ways. Is it undemocratic, for example, to automatically assign a public role to an individual because of her private relationship to an elected official? What limits should be placed on a person with a private relationship to a public official regarding involvement in the public policy making process? How can such individuals be held accountable?

Constraints that have been placed on the presidential spouse's action in the public sphere contradict the liberal tradition of individualism that has characterized American social and political culture. The individual is at the center of liberal democracy, but patriarchy has limited women's opportunities, especially in the public sphere. The family, and not the adult individual, as the basic political unit lies behind the individual rhetoric of liberal philosophers. Because of her position in the family, the first lady is not able to act as an independent individual. She may be credited with political influence, but it is an influence hidden behind a mask of domesticity and treated with considerable suspicion. Hillary Rodham Clinton, building on over twenty years of the women's rights movement, directly challenged that tradition. Understanding public response to that challenge is a major goal of this work.

Given the challenge Hillary Rodham Clinton has posed to the role of first lady and the context of broad changes in women's lives that have occurred in the past quarter century, undertaking an analysis of her evolving relationship with the public is an important scholarly mission. I begin that mission with her odyssey through the campaign of 1992 and people's reaction to it as measured in the public opinion polls.

NOTES

1. I intend to explore the extent to which the suffragists had a vision of women as political leaders in future work.

2. The Congressional Women's Caucus was founded in 1978 and became the Congressional Caucus for Women's Issues in 1981. In 1995, it, along with other "legislative service organizations," lost its right to use congressional staff monies to support itself.

3. Had Hillary Rodham Clinton known about this comment, she might have been able to deflect with humor some of the criticism for her infamous "staying home and baking cookies" remark during the campaign of 1992. There is no evidence that Sarah Polk was chastised for such comments or for her involvement in public affairs.

4. From a contemporary perspective, we should also note Lewis Gould's characterization of Lady Bird Johnson's contribution to the development of a substantive role for first ladies. According to Gould, "Working directly on legislation, rallying grassroots backing for national policy, Lady Bird Johnson demonstrated that a first lady could now do more than serve as a feminine conscience or fact-finder of a presidency. It was now conceivable that she could be a functional and integral part of the office itself" (1985, 535).

5. She won her primary and the general election anyway.

Chapter 3

The Campaign for the White House

Throughout Bill Clinton's tenure as governor of Arkansas, Hillary Rodham Clinton had been his political and policy making partner. When he was defeated for reelection to the governorship after one term, she directed his comeback, even taking his last name as her own to placate irate Arkansas voters who viewed her as an "uppity woman." She often used the term "we" in describing the Clinton administration in Arkansas, and the governor had talked in terms of "our" administration. She acted as an "unpaid troubleshooter, marshalling expert opinion on an assortment of social issues. As the chair of Governor Clinton's Arkansas Education Standards Committee, she held public hearings in every county, helping build consensus for education reform" (Clift, 1992). She was the main wage earner in the family, working as a law partner in the now infamous Arkansas Rose law firm. *The National Law Journal* named her as one of the one hundred most influential lawyers in the country. She also engaged in a number of public service activities, most notably serving as chair of the Children's Defense Fund, and she was appointed to numerous corporate board directorships. Given her career and her resume, when Bill Clinton announced his candidacy for president, the stage was set for a dramatic change in the role of first lady. How the Clintons introduced Hillary to the public, how the media framed this transformation, and how political opponents reacted would condition the public's response to a redefining of the first lady as one of the president's policy advisors.

The Clintons initiated and encouraged the idea early in the campaign that Hillary would be a vital political advisor in the White House and play a prominent policy-making role in a Clinton presidency. The aspiring president explained that if he were elected, "it would be an unprecedented partnership, far more than Franklin Roosevelt and Eleanor" (Sheehy 1992, 144).[1] He stimulated public speculation about an appointment for her to a cabinet post. At fund raisers he would quip "Buy one, get one free." Hillary had said, "If you elect Bill, you get me." Thus, they promoted the notion of a dramatically different partnership to lead the country that the national media quickly picked up. For example, the *Detroit Free Press* heralded her unique position early in the campaign in a January 1992 story headlined "Some Say She's the One Who Should Be President" (Creager 1992).

MEDIA COVERAGE

As Hillary Rodham Clinton established a prominent role in the presidential campaign, she became the subject of innumerable press stories. She became the object of press scrutiny during the 1992 campaign to an extent not faced by any previous contemporary would-be first lady. To say the least, she "engendered spirited public debate" (Cooper 1992). Headlines such as "The Hillary Factor," "The Hillary Problem," "All Eyes on Hillary," and "Hillary Then and Now" led news articles during the campaign.

To establish a sense of the extent of the coverage Hillary received during the campaign, I have surveyed a variety of databases of media articles. Included in this process was the *Readers' Guide to Periodical Literature,* the Proquest electronic database, and the *New York Times* and *The Washington Post* indexes.[2] What follows is not a comprehensive content analysis but rather an overview of media coverage. The Proquest search produced 234 articles under Hillary Clinton between January 1 and November 4, 1992. The focus of the earliest articles tended to deal with allegations of Bill Clinton's infidelity and Hillary's defense of him during the New Hampshire primary campaign. Some saw her as saving his campaign by her performance during a nationally televised interview on *60 Minutes* immediately following the Super Bowl in January. However, she also generated criticism from some quarters for her remark that she was "not sitting here, some little woman standing by my man like Tammy Wynette." Tammy Wynette took great offense at this comment, and Hillary was accused of insulting country music fans. "Many country-western fans—there are millions—took the Wynette remark as an uppity slur on the music they love" (Benedetto 1992). "Mrs. Clinton's putdown of Wynette is only the latest example of why the Democratic party has been losing the country music vote in presidential elections" (Neal 1992). (See also Carroll 1992; Wooten 1992.)

On the other hand, many of the early stories focused on her being an asset to the campaign. For example, the *Chicago Tribune* headlined an article on January 31, "Hillary Clinton May Be Candidate's Top Asset"

(McRoberts and Thomas 1992). These stories were also initial acknowledgement that she would be a different type of first lady. In a Reuters News Service piece headlined "Stand by Your Man? New Look in Campaign Wives," Deborah Zabarenko described "Hillary Clinton as [stepping] forward as one of a new breed of presidential candidates' wives: smart, tough, telegenic and nobody's bimbo" (1992). Other reporters had a difficult time figuring out how to describe the campaigning of this assertive political partner. One of the most mixed characterizations from this period came from Joseph Kahn of the *Boston Globe*. In a February 13 piece titled "As her Husband's Campaign Struggles, She Hits the Hustings in New Hampshire," Kahn characterizes Clinton as "less like the sweetheart of *Sixty Minutes* than a one-woman assault team, arriving by land, air and over frozen water to spray automatic-weapons fire on the Bush administration's domestic policies and political tactics. . . . Charismatic, articulate and accomplished in her own right, the 44-year-old Clinton is shucking the gloves this week and taking on her husband's opponents bareknuckled. To observe her up close during a full (very full) day on the stump is to understand why Arkansas folks are called 'razorbacks'—and why voters repeatedly ask her why she's not running for office herself. . . . On the battlefield of partisan politics, Hillary Clinton is not inclined to take any prisoners" (1992).

In March, the critical stories began in earnest, primarily as a result of her "stay at home and bake cookies and make tea" comment (described more fully below). Discussion about her role and the role of political wives dominated the media during this time frame. In September of the campaign year, Robin Toner in the *New York Times* calculated that "[a]t least twenty articles in major publications this year involved some comparison between Mrs. Clinton and a grim role model for political wives: Lady Macbeth" (1992).

As the campaign progressed and the Clintons headed to the July national convention, we began to get analyses and criticisims of Hillary's political make-over. She seemed to soften her rhetoric and her personal appearance and was showcased in more traditional contexts while attempting to play a more subordinate role to that of her husband. This emphasis continued through the Democratic convention in July. In August, media emphasis switched to coverage and analyses of the Republican attacks on her at their national convention. In the fall, the philosophical discussions about women politicians and political wives continued to a degree. Hillary also obtained coverage on issues and public policy as she gave a number of substantive speeches. She continued to counterattack the Republicans during this period.

Forty-one articles in twenty-four different publications appeared under the heading of Hillary Rodham Clinton between January 1st and the election in November in the *Readers' Guide*. They included three *People Weekly* stories with human interest profiles, highly critical pieces in the arch-conservative *The American Spectator*, and analyses by *U.S. News & World Report, Time,* and *Newsweek.* They included stories in "women's magazines": *Glamour* ("Are We Ready for a First Lady as First Partner?" "Hillary Speaks to Her Mythologizers"), *Ladies Home Journal* ("Hillary Clinton: Road Warrior"), *Vanity Fair* ("What Hillary Wants"), and the more feminist periodicals of *Working Mother* ("Hillary Clinton: Working Mom in the White House?") and *Working Woman* ("The First Lady with a Career?"). The focus of these pieces can be roughly catalogued into six major areas: general analysis (primarily articles in the major news magazines), analyses with a feminist focus, negative analyses of her ideology and career, policy analyses (including reviews of her writings and speeches—mainly positive in content), human interest pieces, and profiles. The purpose of cataloguing the general thrust of these articles is to illustrate the high interest she generated during the campaign and the variety of approaches and angles the media took. The distribution of each type of focus is as follows:

- 7 articles—general analysis
- 7 articles—feminist analysis
- 9 articles—negative analysis
- 5 articles—policy analysis
- 3 articles—human interest
- 9 articles—profiles

A comparison of the number and type of articles about her with those about other presidential candidates' spouses further illustrates her distinctive role in this election. Between January 1992 and November 4, the *New York Times* listed sixty-six references in its index under "Hillary Rodham Clinton," forty-nine of which were under the subheading of "Presidential Election." This number compares with thirty-three references for Barbara Bush or "Mrs. George Bush",[3] seventeen of which were under the "Presidential Election" subheading.[4] Non-presidential-election indexed articles concerning Barbara Bush primarily consisted of reports of trips and other activities as well as discussion of the president. The non-presidential-election indexed articles under Hillary Rodham Clinton centered on issues such as "Children & Youth," "Child Custody & Support," and "Education and Schools," all dealing with her policy focus. Both women had citations under "Bakeries & Baked Products," and "Cookies." The *Washington Post* indexed nineteen stories about Barbara Bush and thirty stories about Hillary Rodham Clinton during this same time frame.

The News Study Group at New York University tracked news coverage of Hillary from the campaign through her first months in the White House. They report that during the presidential primary season when the story of Hillary Rodham Clinton was

> fresh and getting good play, male reporters were likelier to be writing about Hillary Clinton than female reporters (62 stories with male bylines, 58 with female bylines, 30 unattributed).[5] . . . The earliest coverage was likely to be conventional. Syndicated columnist and TV commentator Clarence Page, for example, wrote of the unwritten rules for spouses of political candidates in "Help for the Confused Political Wife" in the March 22, 1992, edition of the Chicago Tribune. Many early stories were also patronizing and/or hostile (according to Dick Williams of the Atlanta Journal-Constitution, Bill Clinton was "married to the radical Left"). In fact, press treatment of Hillary Clinton became a major story. The Clinton campaign, The Washington Post reported, was engaged in an "internal tug-of-war over how to divide Mrs. Clinton's policy-making and cookie baking roles. . . . (Diamond, Gellier, and Ruiz 1993.)

Both male and female reporters have been accused of having a problem covering Clinton. Katha Pollit (1993) described what she viewed as the "Male Media's Hillary Problem" and Katherine Corcoran (1993) took on female reporters in her piece "Pilloried Clinton: Were the Women Who Covered Hillary Clinton During the Campaign Guilty of Sexism?" Pollit attributed the problem to ideological differences, jealousy, and "protection of turf." Male journalists are afraid of losing their jobs to women, she contended. Corcoran said that the "media were confused by Hillary Clinton. Reporters simply didn't know how to write about a post-women's movement, professional baby boomer in line to become first lady."

Some of the media called attention to the larger issues about women's place in society involved in Hillary Clinton's campaigning, and thoughtful articles did appear discussing the contradictions and challenges emanating from her participation in the election. For example, the *New York Times* referenced her as "a lightning rod for the mixed emotions we have about work and motherhood, dreams and accommodation, smart women and men's worlds," and the *Los Angeles Times* commented "[t]he squirming over Hillary Clinton isn't so much about a first lady as about ambivalence over women, power, work and marriage" (Morrison 1992). In "Time for a Feminist as First Lady?" Patt Morrison did a particularly insightful job of laying out the cultural tangles Hillary presented in the campaign. She showed the problem of the modern woman with a substantial resumé of her own playing a supporting role for her husband's ambition rather than achieving a professional goal for herself, and Americans' responses to that role. Overall, the media presented the public with a bewildering array of images and commentary from which to develop a perspective on the candidate's wife and to reflect on an evolving role for first ladies.

POLITICAL OPPOSITION

Political opposition attacked Hillary Rodham Clinton to an extent seldom experienced before by candidates' wives. Historically, first ladies have been vilified after entering the White House. For example, during the Roosevelt re-election campaigns, foes chanted "We don't want Eleanor, either." But few have been the object of political derision as a would-be first lady. Some Republicans had attempted to portray Kitty Dukakis as an unpatriotic radical in the 1988 campaign. Andrew Jackson opponents "advised voters to consider carefully the wisdom of putting Rachel [Jackson] 'at the head of the female society of the United States'." Rachel Jackson's opponents' concern, however, was not her political beliefs but with her moral rectitude to serve as first lady (Caroli 1985).

Republicans launched an anti-Hillary campaign perceived to be so vitriolic that Bill Clinton accused them of making Hillary Clinton the "Willie Horton" of the campaign. Writing in *Commonweal* in October, Abigail McCarthy (1992) reflected, "For good or worse, Hillary Clinton has been made an issue—the Willie Horton issue of 1992." (See, also, Mann's "Hillary Horton?" 1992). In perhaps one of the less biting of the criticisms, former President Richard Nixon warned that her forceful intelligence was likely to make her husband "look like a wimp." Voters, he told reporters, won't accept a man whose wife is "too strong and too intelligent" (*New York Times*, 2/6/92). Republican strategist Roger Ailes chimed in that "Hillary Clinton in an apron was like Michael Dukakis in a tank" (Hall 1992). At their national convention, she was shrilly attacked. Pamphlets depicted her as a "femi-nazi" (Lewis 1992). Patrick Buchanan denounced her as a champion of "radical feminism" and claimed that "Clinton & Clinton" would impose a far-left agenda on the nation" (*New York Times*, August 20, 1992). Richard Bond, chair of the Republican National Committee "caricatured Hillary Clinton as a law-suit mongering feminist who likened marriage to slavery and encouraged children to sue their parents" (Ifill 1992a). Pat Robertson accused Bill and Hillary Clinton of "talking about a radical plan to destroy the traditional family and transfer its functions to the federal government" (Germond and Witcover 1993, 412).

The attacks perhaps reached their zenith in the national convention speech of Marilyn Quayle, which was viewed as going too far. The attacks backfired on the Republicans. According to Marilyn Quayle, "Not everyone [in her generation] believed that the family was so oppressive that women could only thrive apart from it." One line that made negative headlines was "They [liberals] are disappointed because most women do not wish to be liberated from their essential natures as women. Most of us love being mothers and wives." Just as Hillary Clinton earlier had been criticized for seeming to put down full-time homemakers, Marilyn Quayle appeared to attack women who had careers outside the home. Kathleen Hall Jamieson, Dean of the Annenberg School of Journalism at the University of Pennsylvania, found in a series of focus groups that the "essential natures" phrase was retained by women to a striking degree. According to Dean Jamieson, "The level of hostility toward [Marilyn Quayle] and that speech was very high. I think there was some resentment at someone standing up and telling women what choices are and are not appropriate for them" (Toner 1992). While this speech was an attack on liberals in general, it was widely viewed as an attack indirectly aimed at Hillary Clinton.

HILLARY AND THE CAMPAIGN

How was it that Hillary Rodham Clinton became a controversial figure in the campaign? There were defining moments in the campaign for her, and for the most part they were not pleasant. Her main introduction to the public was the *60 Minutes* interview in which she had to express support for and defend her supposedly philandering husband. That interview, although a very difficult and embarrassing situation, seemed to generate a positive response from the public, not withstanding the backlash over the Tammy Wynette comment.

But then came her infamous "stay home and bake cookies" remark. In response to a charge from Jerry Brown, a primary opponent of her husband's, that her law firm had benefited unfairly from her marriage to the governor of Arkansas, she commented "I suppose I could have stayed home and baked cookies and had teas." This line was widely quoted and seemed to be a put-down of women who chose to stay at home. It stroked the culture gap fires that had been a problem for the women's movement throughout its history. It "aroused hostility among traditional women who saw it as a condemnation of their life choices" (Campbell 1993, 4). (For a review of how this comment became a media issue, see Jamieson 1995.) However, this statement was only part of Hillary's response to Brown's charge. "I chose to fulfill my profession, which I had before my husband was in public life. The work that I have done as a professional, a public advocate, has been aimed . . . to assure that women can make the choices . . . whether it's full-time career, full-time motherhood or some combination," she had continued in the interview. The full context of her response suggests a more balanced reflection on the difficult decisions women have faced. But the media chose to ignore that.

The opposition also tore apart her earlier writings in law journals about children's rights. As several commentators have noted, this policy element of the debate engendered by Hillary on the campaign trail represented a turning point in commentary about first ladies: she was not being criticized for her clothes or her social life but for her public policy stances. As Richard Cohen of *The Washington Post* put it "Something truly remarkable had happened. A spouse was being attacked not for the way she was dressed or (as with Nancy Reagan) where she was getting those dresses from, but for her views, for her writings, for her speeches . . ."(1992). As Suzanne Garment put it in the *Los Angeles Times*, ". . . there is something unusual about the criticism of Hillary Clinton. She is being attacked not for her character or her finances but for her views and positions. This is, we must suppose, a step forward" (1992). Further, in a move "unheard of" for a prospective first lady, Clinton was invited to a breakfast interview at *The Washington Post* where she was asked questions of a substantive nature (Corcoran 1993). Hillary Clinton had added a substantive focus to the campaign, however controversial, that citizens were able to reflect upon for the first time.

THE PEOPLE'S VIEW IN THE CAMPAIGN

Media attention given to the aspiring first lady during the campaign included charting the people's impressions of Hillary Rodham Clinton through national surveys as her fortune waxed and waned. The polls were often an integral part of a news story's development. For example, *Vanity Fair* commissioned a poll by Yankelovich, Clancy, and Shulman for a major article by Gail Sheehy, a writer who had gained prominence writing psychological profiles of other national political figures. That poll included the public's general reaction to Hillary Clinton, whether she should pursue a separate career as first lady, and a battery of items on her personal characteristics (Sheehy 1992).[6]

U.S. News & World Report concluded as early as April 1992 that their poll "show[ed] that Americans are sharply divided over Hillary Clinton. Forty-six percent of respondents say that she would make a good or excellent first lady . . . and that's well below the 77 percent who think Barbara Bush is doing a good or excellent job."[7] Near the end of the campaign, however, Donnie Radcliffe in *The Washington Post* concluded that ". . . the polls indicate she is no longer a liability to Bill Clinton; in a variety of surveys, her "negatives" are down from their startlingly high levels of the spring. She's no Barbara Bush, but she doesn't appear to be a drag on the ticket either" (Cooper 1992).

How extensive were the polls during the campaign, to what degree did they show a public polarized in their opinion of Hillary Rodham Clinton, and to what extent was she viewed negatively? What did they indicate about her base of support and opposition? The earliest poll, one conducted by Yankelovich in February, not surprisingly found that the majority of the public had not yet formed an opinion. Sixty-five percent said they were either unfamiliar with Hillary Clinton or unsure of their opinion. Twenty-six percent had a favorable opinion and 9 percent were unfavorable.

By March, Gallup (for *USA TODAY*), CBS/NYT and *The Washington Post* had all begun to ask the public about its impressions of Hillary Clinton. CBS/NYT, and *The Washington Post* found 31 percent and 28 percent, respectively, having a favorable opinion while 17 percent and 22 percent, respectively, had a negative opinion. The majority had no opinion in *The Washington Post* poll. Gallup reported a more highly crystallized opinion base: 39 percent were favorable and 26 percent were unfavorable in March of 1992. By April, Yankelovich found negative impressions doubling to 19 percent from the 9 percent in February, while favorable impressions dropped one point to 25 percent. Another poll at the end of March shows something quite different. *Newsweek* had commissioned the Gallup organization to do a national poll. The results were reported in a sidebar to a March 30 article titled "Will Hillary Hurt or Help?" In this poll people were asked, "What is your overall impression of Hillary Clinton, Bill Clinton's wife: favorable or unfavorable?" Sixty-five percent said "favorable" and 16 percent responded "unfavorable." This is an extraordinarily high rating hardly suggesting that Hillary had become a liability to the campaign. But nowhere in the article are the poll results discussed. The article states, however, that the "core issue, arguably, is whether America is really ready for a self-confident, politically active woman like Hillary Clinton as first lady" (Carroll 1992, 31). The poll seemed to have answered that question in the affirmative for the moment.

Given that voters usually do not focus their attention on the campaign for the presidency until the fall of the election year (although their opinions are extensively measured from the earliest days of the campaign), these polls show an unusually fast decline in respondents expressing "no opinion" on this future first lady. Figure 3.1 shows average favorable and unfavorable ratings for Hillary during the 1992 campaign months across the available polls.[8] Her highest favorable ratings were the 65 percent obtained in the Gallup Poll for *Newsweek* cited above and in a September Gallup Poll when 56 percent expressed a favorable opinion of her. Her highest negative rating was 33 percent obtained in the *U.S. News & World Report* April survey.

Generally about one-third to 40 percent of the public had a favorable opinion, and about one-fifth to one-quarter had an unfavorable impression of Hillary Rodham Clinton during the campaign. The only comparison we

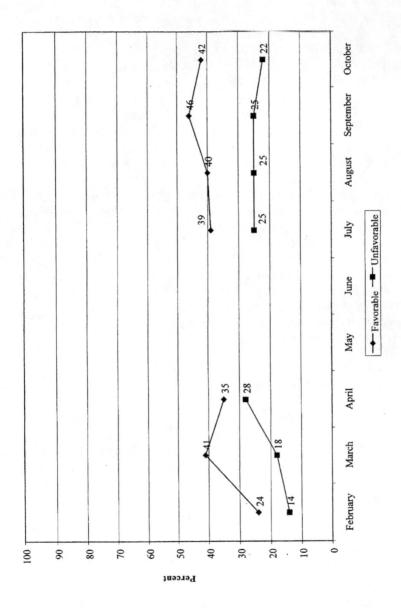

Fig. 3.1. Average Favorable and Unfavorable Ratings, Hillary Rodham Clinton, 1992 Campaign.

have from previous presidential elections is an October 1988 NBC poll on Barbara Bush and Kitty Dukakis. In that poll, 48 percent of a sample of likely voters had a favorable opinion of Barbara Bush, 11 percent were unfavorable and 41 percent were unsure. Kitty Dukakis was viewed favorably by 42 percent, unfavorably by 11 percent, and 47 percent were unsure of their opinion of her. Thus, positive opinions of Hillary compared favorably with these previous candidates' wives, but her negative ratings were also somewhat higher. Because of her prominent position in the campaign, people were more familiar with her and had more definite opinions about her than they had had of candidates' wives in previous elections.

Polls were not the only method through which politicians gleaned a sense of public opinion about Hillary Clinton. She was also the subject of focus groups conducted by both sides in the campaign. The Clinton campaign also used a dial group.[9] In the spring of the campaign, the dial group showed that Hillary was not helping the campaign. "The readings fell precipitously at the mere sight of her face on-screen" (Goldman et al. 1994: 255). In the focus groups, as reported by Clinton's pollster Stan Greenberg, "people [thought] of her as being in the race 'for herself' and as 'going for the power.' She is not seen as particularly 'family-oriented.' More than Nancy Reagan, she is seen as 'running the show'" (Goldman et al. 1994: 251).

In an April 27 report, Clinton advisers wrote that "Hillary should have a lower profile in the immediate short-term, as we try to reintroduce Bill Clinton. . . . After a short pull-back period, Hillary needs to come forward in a way that is much more reflective of herself—both her humor and her advocacy work for children. . . . Bill and Hillary need to clarify Hillary's role as first lady. Ambiguity looks like a power game. It is very important that voters feel comfortable with Hillary's role and not see her as an empowered Nancy Reagan" (Goldman et al. 1994: 663).

Clinton operatives saw the negative view of Hillary changing by the end of the Democratic convention. In a memo to Bill Clinton, Stan Greenberg reported:

> Hillary Clinton's favorability has risen steadily in this period, paralleling the gains for Bill Clinton. Her mean favorability stood at 41.7 degrees [on a 0–100 "thermometer scale"] before Gore, but rose steadily to 50 degrees and a net positive by Wednesday night. Moreover, there was an utterly new reaction to Hillary in the dial groups. In June, the mean line usually dropped down when Hillary appeared on the screen, but at the convention Thursday night that all changed: the line held steady or moved up (Goldman et al. 1994: 702).

GROUP SUPPORT AND OPPOSITION

Early in the campaign it was apparent that Hillary would be more popular with some groups of people than others and that the media would highlight these differences. For example, the *USA TODAY* headline regarding its March poll read "Women, Young Rate Hillary Clinton Highest" (Castaneda and O'Connell 1992). Original data from two sets of national 1992 campaign surveys provide the opportunity to examine in more detail the polarizing nature of Hillary Rodham Clinton in that election. I use these data to explore who her supporters and detractors were and to gain a perspective on the cultural bases of her support. The data sets are the American National Election Study (ANES) conducted by the University of Michigan and two CBS/NYT polls.

For the first time in their series of election studies, the 1992 ANES included the potential first ladies in their "feeling thermometer" questions about political leaders and other people in the news.[10] How warmly did people feel about Hillary Clinton? Nine percent of survey respondents said they could not rate Hillary Clinton on the feeling thermometer scale because they did not know enough about her or did not recognize her name. Twenty-six percent rated her at 50 degrees, feeling neither warm not cold, while 43 percent felt warm toward her (rating their feelings above 50 degrees on the scale) and 23 percent felt cold (rating her below 50 degrees).[11] Her mean thermometer rating was 55 degrees. Bill Clinton's was 56 degrees. Respondents tended to feel both colder (30 percent) and warmer (56 percent) toward the candidate than his wife.

Two July and August CBS/NYT polls are pooled together for analysis purposes.[12] These polls asked respondents "Is your opinion of Hillary Clinton favorable, not favorable, undecided, or haven't you heard enough about Hillary Clinton yet to have an opinion?" In these polls, over one-half of the respondents were either undecided or had not heard enough to form a judgment, 33 percent were favorable, and 16 percent were unfavorable.

Men and women did not diverge in their response to the future first lady at this point. Women expressed only a slightly greater degree of warmth than men in the ANES study. The average feeling thermometer score was 56 degrees for women and 53 degrees for men. The CBS polls also showed no sex differences in attitudes at this stage. Thirty-three percent of women and 32 percent of men were favorable. In post-1994 election analyses, "angry white males" were seen as dominating that election. Hillary Rodham Clinton was viewed as a target of their anger. But during the 1992 election it was not disproportionately white men who expressed the most intense dislike for her. To test the hypothesis of greater antipathy on the part of white men, respondents in the ANES study were divided into two groups: those who rated Hillary Clinton on the thermometer at 20 degrees or lower and those who rated her above 20 degrees. Ten percent of white men and nine percent of everyone else rated her at the "frigid" end of the scale.

Blacks were substantially more positive than whites on the ANES thermometer. Blacks had an average score of 62 degrees, while whites had a score of 54 degrees. Thirty-five percent of blacks and 33 percent of whites were favorable towards Hillary Clinton in the CBS polls. Whites were more likely to be unfavorable and less likely to be undecided than blacks. Sixteen percent of whites compared with 6 percent of blacks said they were unfavorable, while 59 percent of blacks and 51 percent of whites were undecided.

Age, education, and income had little impact on feeling thermometer scores for the future first lady. In the CBS polls, 40- to 49-year-olds were above the average in their favorable opinions—40 percent compared with the overall average of 33 percent. They were less likely to be undecided and as likely to be unfavorable as other age groups. But other age groups did not deviate from the overall average. People with different amounts of formal education and different levels of income tended to rate her similarly.

Not unexpectedly, party affiliation was strongly related to feelings toward Hillary Clinton. Democrats had an average thermometer score of 65, Republicans had an average score of 43, and independents tended to rate her at 54 degrees. In statistical terms, the correlation between ratings on the ANES thermometer and strength of party identification was .47 ($p = .001$), a quite strong relationship. Party affiliation was also the major factor dividing positive from negative opinions in the CBS polls. Democrats, Republicans, and independents were equally likely to be undecided—51 percent of each group. But 41 percent of self-identified Democrats compared with 34 percent of independents and only 24 percent of Republicans reported being favorably disposed toward the would-be first lady. Nearly one-quarter of Republicans said they were unfavorable (24 percent); only 8 percent of Democrats felt this way and 15 percent of independents felt this way.

Table 3.1 presents the coefficients from a multivariate analysis of the CBS and ANES data to test more precisely the relationship between these sociodemographic factors and impressions of Hillary Clinton. In multivariate analysis, we examine how a set of variables jointly affect another variable, in this case the effect of sociodemographic factors—age, education, race, income, sex and party affiliation—on the public's attitude toward Hillary Clinton during the 1992 campaign. Support, for example, may be a function of both one's age and education. In multivariate analysis, we can examine the impact of one variable taking into account (or controlling for) the effect of other variables. Thus, for example, how do people in the same age group but with different levels of education differ in their support for Hillary? The coefficients presented show the relative strength of each relationship controlling for all of the others.

In the multivariate analysis of the ANES data, these variables (age, education, income, sex, race, and strength of party identification) explained 21 percent of the variance in feelings toward Hillary Clinton, with only party strength proving significant as a variable (Table 3.1).[13] The multivariate analysis of the CBS polls in Table 3.1 examines supporters and nonsupporters. Undecideds are excluded. The CBS model is estimated using logit regression because of the dichotomous dependent variable. As with the ANES data, analysis of the CBS poll data found only party affiliation having a statistically significant effect on attitudes toward Hillary Clinton. Democrats were her strong supporters while Republicans, not surprisingly, were her detractors. Men and women seemed not to be viewing her in very different lights, nor was there a clash among age groups or classes. The coefficient for sex is negative, indicating men were slightly more favorable of Hillary at this time, controlling for all the other factors (and with undecideds excluded).

In a separate logistic regression analysis of the CBS polls examining the difference between undecideds and those expressing an opinion (regardless of whether it was negative or positive), undecideds were more likely to be younger persons with less education and less income. No statistically significant difference existed between the sexes. Republicans were not more undecided than others, nor were Democrats more opinionated.

Table 3.1. Multivariate Analysis of Group Support for Hillary Clinton

Factor	ANES survey (standardized regression coefficients)	CBS poll (Logit regression coefficients)
Sex	.006	−.07
Age	.02	−.01
Income	−.02	.04
Education	.009	.04
Race	.01	.47
Party Strength	−.45	NA
Democrat	NA	1.01**
Republican	NA	−.79**
Adjusted R^2 = .21		

** p = .001
Race was coded 0 = white, 1 = black; sex was coded 0 = male, 1 = female; party strength went from 1 = strong Democrat to 7 = strong Republican.

To summarize, these data show that Hillary Clinton was viewed primarily as a partisan figure during the 1992 campaign. Differences that we might have expected to be reflected in age, education, and sex in support did not appear.

In addition to the effects of partisan factors, we should expect that political attitudes would separate supporters from opponents of this potential first lady and that, especially, proponents of women's rights would be among Hillary's advocates. Sapiro and Conover (1993) have tested the impact of these factors on affect for Hillary Clinton. Using the ANES data, Sapiro and Conover developed a much more inclusive model than that presented in Table 3.1—19 variables in all—including a number of economic perspectives, values, and issue positions as well as demographic and partisan factors. In their model, variance explained the amount of variation in support increased to 31 percent with partisanship and affect toward her spouse by far the most substantial contributors to that variance. The Hill–Thomas hearings and the issues of abortion and moralism also produced statistically significant differences among respondents in their feelings toward Hillary Clinton.

In the end, what effect did Hillary Rodham Clinton have on the election of 1992? How large a role did she play in the campaign as whole? Did she have an impact on voters? To address the first question, we can peruse the literature on the campaign. In their analysis of the election in *The Election of 1992*, political scientist Gerald Pomper and his colleagues barely mention Hillary Clinton. She is not referenced in the index, and the visibility that created much media attention for her is not examined. However, in *Democracy's Feast: Elections in America*, edited by political scientist Herbert Weisberg, which analyzes the 1992 election from a scholarly perspective, a chapter is devoted to "The Candidates' Wives" (Mughan and Burden, 1995). The chapter analyzes the same "thermometer score" data from the ANES study. I have noted earlier that the wives of the candidates were included for the first time because of Hillary Clinton's challenge to traditional gender roles. Thus, her presence was the initial catalyst that made "The Candidates Wives" a component of *Democracy's Feast*.

Turning to the work of journalists, we find that Jack Germond and Jules Witcover's *Mad as Hell* (1993), a chronology and analysis of the election as a whole does not have her playing a defining role. This work only peripherally mentions her problems and influence. But she was clearly a major presence in the development of Clinton campaign strategy as reflected in the overview of the campaign by Goldman et al. in *Quest for the Presidency: 1992* (1994). These authors had access to the daily operations of the Clinton effort, and Hillary's presence loomed large from that angle. Also, as shown earlier, she was the subject of media stories to a much greater extent than other candidates' wives. She received prime coverage in national news magazines and was interviewed by the editorial staff of a major national newspaper. We must conclude that her centrality to the history of the election was somewhat unprecedented but variable as observed from the lens of expert campaign observers—both academic and journalistic.

Her effect on the voters was also noted in the campaign. In April, interestingly at a point when Hillary appeared to be a campaign liability, "the Gallup Organization calculated the Hillary Factor in a race between Clinton and Bush. Making an admittedly 'rough' analysis, Gallup Vice President Larry Hugick said the Hillary effect actually meant a gain for her husband of 1.6 percent" (Corcoran 1993). Mughan and Burden (1995), in their analysis of the influence of the candidates' wives on votes for their husbands in 1992 using the ANES data I have used above, concluded that Hillary Rodham Clinton was an electoral asset to her husband. A multivariate analysis showed that affect for Hillary had a statistically significant positive effect on the vote for Bill Clinton. Thus, in the end, rather than being a drag on the ticket, she seemed to help her husband, at least as indicated by certain pieces of statistical data.

The campaign certainly posed problems in reconciling the role of first lady, or that of the spouse of president, with greater equality and individual achievement for women. The people's response to Hillary Clinton and debate about private and public roles were distinctive phenomena of the campaign. There is no doubt that she rates high in the folklore of the 1992 election. She forced attention on women's roles in American society in new ways. I turn now to an examination of what happened to people's perspectives once she entered the White House and began transforming the first ladyship. These changes will have a lasting impact on how women can achieve in the political realm.

NOTES

1. The candidate's words may have been a calculated effort to attract the more liberal primary votes of the Democratic Party.

2. Since some articles from the latter two sources are included in the Proquest compilation, duplication exists, and the reader should not just add together the results of this survey.

3. This is the way her name was referenced in the newspaper index.

4. In 1988, the *New York Times* indexed twenty-nine stories about Kitty Dukakis, wife of the Democratic nominee, Michael Dukakis, seven of which were about her health problems. Barbara Bush rated six references in that year's index.

5. This group does not present any data regarding the distribution of male and female reporters covering the election. It may be that female reporters were disproportionately getting bylines on Hillary Clinton relative to their presence.

6. See Chapter 6 in *Public Opinion, the First Ladyship and Hillary Rodham Clinton* for findings on public perceptions of her personal characteristics.

7. What they don't tell readers is the percentage of respondents who thought Hillary would make a poor first lady and how many said "don't know" to the ques-

tion. Just comparing the favorable responses at this early stage of introducing Hillary Rodham Clinton to the public does not tell the whole story.

8. The polls included were Gallup, Yankelovich, *The Washington Post*/ABC, CBS/NYT, NBC/WSJ, and *Newsweek*. The average in different months varies in part because the different pollsters used different questions. Question wording has an effect of the distribution of responses. A discussion of this effect is presented in the next chapter.

9. The dial technique involves assembling a group of people in a room, showing them a video presentation of ads and speeches, and asking them to register their responses by turning a dial on a handheld electronic meter (Goldman et al. 1994: 255).

10. Interviewees are told that "ratings between 50 degrees and 100 degrees mean that you feel favorable and warm toward the person. Ratings between 0 degrees and 50 degrees mean that you don't feel favorable toward the person and that you don't care too much for that person. You would rate the person at the 50 degree mark if you don't feel particularly warm or cold toward the person. If we come to a person whose name you don't recognize, you don't need to rate that person." The inclusion of Hillary Clinton and Barbara Bush in the feeling thermometers resulted from interest in gender and feminism issues among ANES officials which led to the inclusion of a question on Hillary. Barbara Bush was then included for balance, according to Virginia Sapiro of the Board of Directors of ANES.

11. The remainder of the respondents in the survey said they were not able to rate her.

12. The percentages do not add to 100 percent because of rounding.

13. Significance here refers to statistical significance, which indicates how confident we are that if we could measure the opinions of the whole population and not just a sample that a relationship would exist between the variable.

Chapter 4

Public Perceptions of the First Lady

GENERAL IMPRESSIONS OF HILLARY RODHAM CLINTON AS FIRST LADY

Hillary Rodham Clinton's activities on the campaign trail in 1992 stimulated a new domain of questioning for public opinion pollsters. Prior to the 1992 election surveying the public about their impressions of presidential wives and the job they were doing was a sporadic undertaking for pollsters. As we have seen in Chapter 3, people's impressions of Hillary Clinton was a frequent subject of polls during the 1992 election. In the first two years of the Clinton administration, just as every month the public was asked how they felt the president was doing, they were asked about the first lady. Polling about the first lady after the first two years was somewhat more sporadic but still quite extensive.

Newspaper headlines chronicled the continuing story of the first lady's popularity during the Clinton presidency. Hillary Rodham Clinton began her tenure as a popular first lady. Headlines in state newspapers proclaimed her popularity among their citizens: "Hillary Clinton's Support Booms" headlined the *Tennessee Commercial Appeal* in March 1993; the *Cincinnati Post* reported "First Lady Rates High in Ohio" in May 1993; in Iowa, the *Des Moines Register* headlined "Iowans Give Thumbs Up to First Lady." Nationally we find such headlines as "Activist Role Wins Approval" and "The President Is Clearly in Second Place" (*USA TODAY* October 1 and 5, 1993). Headlines continuously showed trends in public response as she faced scrutiny over the failed health care plan, Whitewater events, and, later, her reemergence as a positive figure during the last years of the Clinton presidency. Examples include: "First Lady's Softer Focus Follows Drop in Popularity" (*Washington Post*, 10/15/95), "First Lady

Bears Brunt of Unfavorable Opinion on Whitewater" (*Washington Post*, 3/24/96), "First Lady Finds Positive Image as She Turns 50" (*Wisconsin State Journal*), "Hillary Clinton Zooms in Public Esteem" (*The Capital Times*, 8/11/98), and "Hillary Clinton: Popular and Hardly in Hiding" (*New York Times*, 8/12/98). *The Gallup Poll Monthly* also captures the saga of Hillary's relationship to the people. Gallup's series on her received such titles as "Hillary Clinton Maintains Public Support" (April 1994), "First Lady a Growing Liability for Clinton," (January 1996) and "First Lady's Popularity Rebounds" (January 1997).

This chapter chronicles and analyzes the people's responses to Hillary Rodham Clinton as first lady using the findings of these many and varied polls as the basis for measurement. Questions explored in this chapter primarily focus on how popular she has been and how the public has rated the job she has done as first lady. Chapter 5 then explores in depth the public's reaction to her attempt to transform the first ladyship into more of a public policy advisory role within the executive branch.

In anticipation of her taking on the job of first lady, *U.S. News & World Report* asked the public in January 1993: "What kind of a job do you think Hillary Clinton will do as first lady?" Seventy-two percent thought she would do either an excellent (30 percent) or a good (42 percent) job, while 18 percent felt she would do only a fair job and five percent thought she would do a poor job (Walsh 1993).

In the first edition of *Public Opinion, the First Ladyship and Hillary Rodham Clinton,* I explained how pollsters' wording of questions often affect the responses they get. The wording of questions about people's impressions of Hillary Clinton as first lady has influenced how popular she has appeared to be. It has mattered especially whether a survey has explicitly invited respondents to say they were undecided in response to a question about their impressions of her. In Hillary's case, the CBS/NYT polls have consistently had a smaller portion of respondents making a judgement about her than the Gallup Poll. The CBS/NYT polls include a "don't know" option in their question wording. (See Figure 4.2) They do not leave it as a volunteered response. "Experimental research shows that many more people will say 'don't know' when that alternative is explicitly offered than when it is not" (Converse and Presser 1986, 35). This option lowered both her positive and negative ratings when we compare CBS/NYT findings with those of Gallup.

The first edition of this book presented poll results on Hillary Rodham Clinton's favorability ratings for the first two years of the Clinton presidency. It examined the rise and fall in her popularity across various polls. Here I expand the trend line into 1999, covering a more than six-year period. Four measures are used to assess trends in the public's impressions of Hillary Clinton during this time and give us a multi-faceted perspective:

Gallup polls and CBS/NYT polls regarding her favorability ratings, polls asking about approval of the job she was doing, and thermometer scale ratings from the 1994, 1996, and 1998 American National Election Studies (see Chapter 3). Figures 4.1 and 4.2 show the trend in Hillary's favorability ratings from 1992 into 1999 in the Gallup Poll and the CBS/NYT polls. The Gallup Poll data used to construct figures were made available through the Roper Center archives at the University of Connecticut. The CBS/NYT data were obtained from the Interuniversity Consortium for Political and Social Research at the University of Michigan.

THE FIRST YEAR

Hillary Rodham Clinton's favorability ratings were high as the Clintons entered the White House in January 1993; 67 percent of the public had a favorable impression in the Gallup Poll.[1] Her support declined somewhat by the 100 days mark , but it increased again by the end of September at the time of her testimony on the Clinton health care plan before Senate and House committees. Sixty-one percent expressed a favorable opinion in the Gallup Poll at that time. Based on average Gallup poll ratings throughout the year, we can say that she won favorable ratings from over one-half of the public in the first few months of the administration and sustained a positive response from approximately the same percentage throughout the rest of the year. Her unfavorable ratings inched up over the course of the year from less than 20 percent to approximately 30 percent The following *Redbook* quote illustrates the change from the 1992 campaign to the White House in Hillary Rodham Clinton's popularity.

> These days, though, nobody has a bad word to say about Hillary Clinton. Call it a honeymoon period (her postelection approval ratings have soared), call it collective amnesia, but for the moment, the first lady can do no wrong. Which is a starkly different picture from last year, when she could do nothing right (Roberts, 1993).

At the end of 1993, in their news release reporting results of their December poll, the Times Mirror Center for the People and the Press declared "Hillary's a Hit." "Positive reviews of Hillary Clinton's job performance run well ahead of evaluations made of the president," the release stated (December 9, 1993). She received a 62 percent approval rating for her handling of her duties as first lady, while 48 percent approved of the job the president was doing. *Vogue* also weighed in noting her triumph:

> This, after all, is Hillary Clinton's moment. . . . She has. . . . captivated Capitol Hill, and she may well guide her husband through his first real legislative victory. Her numbers in the polls are much higher than his; when he

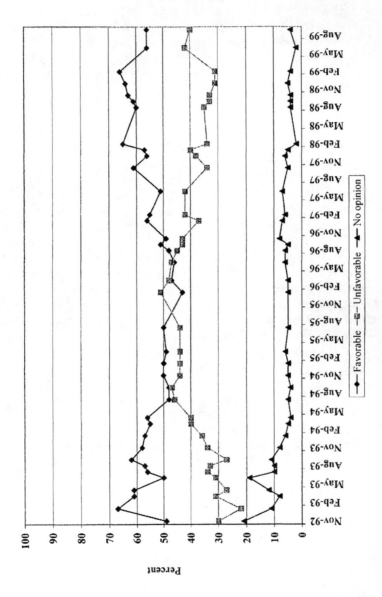

Fig. 4.1. Favorability Ratings for Hillary Rodham Clinton. Do you have a favorable or unfavorable opinion or have you ever heard of Hillary Clinton? Gallup Polls.

unveiled the health-care plan in front of Congress and the nation, it was she, seated in the audience between Tipper Gore and new best friend C. Everett Koop, who got two standing ovations. Her testimony to the House committees on Energy and Commerce and Ways and Means turned into a lovefest that ended in applause. . . . "This is as big as it comes," an aide said before she went on. "This is Eleanor Roosevelt time" (Reed 1993).

THE SECOND YEAR

At the close of the first year of the Clinton administration, a time during which she had played a major public policy advisory role but had also worked to promote an image of herself performing the traditional family and hostess role, journalists were describing Hillary Rodham Clinton as the "very popular" first lady. The story was very different in 1994. The Clintons were hit with major attacks concerning their role in what had come to be called the "Whitewater affair." Questions about Governor Bill Clinton's and Hillary Clinton's financial dealings involving the private land development in Arkansas called Whitewater emerged during the 1992 presidential election but faded from public view. But investigations into the matter had continued into the Clinton presidency. It reemerged on the national scene after the suicide of presidential aide Vincent Foster, and in early January 1994 stories surrounding it dominated in the national news media. As Johnson and Broder describe it, "By the end of those first two weeks in January, Whitewater had taken on a life of its own. It dominated the news to such an extent that the *Washington Post*'s 'National Weekly Edition' devoted its full first page to a bold headline 'WHITEWATER,' with a subhead 'More Questions than Answers'" (1996, 263). The first lady was viewed as a key player in the affair and the media attention on her role seriously undermined the public's confidence in her and her ability to focus national attention on health care reform. That month, President Clinton was forced to ask Attorney General Janet Reno to appoint a special prosecutor to investigate this matter.

The Clintons were slow to respond and lost momentum on public policy concerns as their attention was diverted to defending themselves on this issue. Thus, in the fall of 1994 the administration's health care bill, which was meant to be a centerpiece of the first administration, was withdrawn from consideration by Congress. Hillary Rodham Clinton was seen as being instrumental in its defeat. In the election of 1994, she was often the target of attacks by conservatives, especially talk show hosts who dominated the campaign. As Figure 4.1 shows, her favorability ratings declined to where less than one-half of the public was expressing support and as nearly as large a percentage was expressing disapproval. CBS News in their press release of their November 27–28, 1994 poll captures the change:

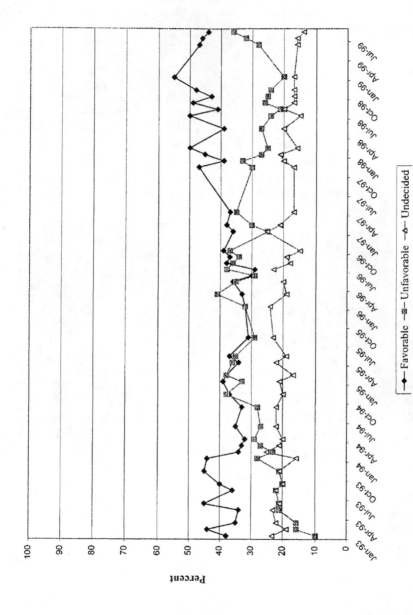

Fig. 4.2. Favorability ratings for Hillary Rodham Clinton, NYT/CBS Polls. Is your opinion of Hillary Rodham Clinton favorable, not favorable, undecided, or haven't you heard enough about Hillary Rodham Clinton yet to have an opinion? NYT/CBS Polls.

Opinions of the first lady have changed for the worse in recent months, with Americans now as likely to view her unfavorably as favorably. More than half of the public say Hillary Rodham Clinton should NOT be in a policy-making role. This is a reversal of Americans' reactions when she was first asked to chair the health care reform commission. In fact the public narrow-ly says her handling of the health care commission was NOT a reason health care reform did not pass last session.

Overall opinion about the first lady in this poll differs by party and by gender. Republicans are two to one negative; Democrats are as overwhelm-ingly positive. Women are favorable; men are not. White men seem especial-ly negative towards Hillary Clinton. Only 38 percent of them hold a favor-able view of the first lady, while 59 percent are unfavorable (CBS News Press Release, 11/29/94).

RISE AND FALL IN POPULARITY DURING THE MIDDLE YEARS

In 1995, the first lady adopted a lower profile, focusing her efforts on advocating for women's and children's issues outside of a formal adminis-tration position. She also began her international trips including her wide-ly publicized speech on women's rights as human rights at the Fourth International Conference on Women's Rights in Beijing, China. (See Chapter 7.) Unfortunately, for an analysis of trends in the people's impres-sions of her, neither Gallup nor CBS/NYT asked about Hillary in their polls during the latter half of 1995, nor was the public's response to her China speech measured.

By the end of 1995, the first lady seemed to have regained a good degree of her popularity. The Times Mirror poll at the end of October found 58 percent of a national sample rating their impressions of her as either very (14 percent) or mostly (44 percent) favorable, while 48 percent were most-ly (24 percent) or very (14 percent) unfavorable. In early December a Yankelovich poll conducted for *Time* magazine and CNN, 57 percent responded that they had a favorable impression while 33 percent were unfavorable. Ann Devroy (1995a) had reported in the *Washington Post* in September 1995 her rating on the "temperature scale" of one to 100 was 44 percent, eight points behind the president, it had increased in December to 52 points.

In January 1996, Hillary Clinton's book *It Takes a Village and Other Lessons Children Teach Us*, a discussion of children and child-rearing issues, arrived at book stores. She was to take a national tour to promote it. This undertaking was to enhance the first lady's image as a strong advo-cate for children and keep a high profile for her on a safe issue. But this effort was deeply undercut when long-missing billing records from her Arkansas law firm suddenly turned up in the White House residence of the first family, raising questions about how much work she had done for the

Madison Guaranty Savings and Loan. Copies of these billing records had long been sought by investigators in the Whitewater affair. The amount of time reported—60 hours—was open to interpretation as to whether it contradicted her earlier testimony of little involvement. The strange way in which they suddenly appeared instilled suspicions about the truthfulness of previous statements.

To make matters worse for the first lady, a memorandum by former White House staff member David Watkins came to light at the same time, strongly suggesting Hillary Rodham Clinton had been a central figure in the firing of the Travel Office staff. Mr. Watkins had written "we both knew that there would be hell to pay if we failed to take swift and decisive action in conformity with the first lady's wishes . . ." (Johnston 1996).

Both the media and the Senate investigating committee jumped on these discoveries and Hillary once again came under heavy criticism. At this time she was also subpoenaed to appear before a grand jury in connection with the Madison Guaranty case. Her political opponents stepped up their vilification of her, most prominently when William Safire in the *New York Times* called her a "congenital liar" (1996). Others wondered about her unprecedented role in the presidential advisory system, and her status among the American public fell.

In January 1996, approximately sixty-two questions were asked of national samples of the public about Hillary Clinton, a number nearly equal to all that had been asked in 1995.[1] In a January 26 report of its January 12–15 poll, *USA TODAY* found 51 percent of those surveyed saying they had an unfavorable opinion of her: "the first time a majority . . . rated her negatively. She received her lowest favorable rating ever, at 43 percent" (Page 1996). Half of women polled, 51 percent, gave her a favorable rating, compared with only 35 percent of men. Younger women and single women liked her most; married men and affluent men liked her least, the article reported. Black voters were much more favorable to her than whites. While their numbers in the survey were small and thus statistically less reliable, 81 percent of black women and 74 percent of black men gave her a favorable rating.

After she testified before the grand jury on January 26, only 25 percent of a national sample thought she was telling the whole truth about Whitewater while twice as many (52 percent) believed she was hiding something. Several polls throughout January found that a majority believed she was lying or covering up something in the Whitewater investigation. A majority also though she was lying about her role in the Travel Office firings.

Her favorability ratings in the Times Mirror poll fell from 58 percent in the previous October to 42 percent in their January 12 1996 survey and her unfavorable rating rose to 54 percent. Her favorability rating fell 12 points in CBS/NYT polls in the first week of January as the new allegations were revealed. In a poll conducted January 2–3, 59 percent of 619 respondents said they had a favorable opinion of the first lady. When the same people were surveyed again on January 10, only 47 percent said they had the same positive opinion. "Those who had a change of mind attributed it to articles on Whitewater or said they were not quite sure why" (Purdum 1996). The downward spiral continued. The nadir for the first lady in the CBS/NYT polls occurred in June 1996 when only 29 percent expressed a favorable opinion and 38 percent had an unfavorable impression.

THE FIRST LADY'S POPULARITY RETURNS

During the 1996 campaign and through 1997 her favorable ratings began to climb in these and other polls and continued a slow upward swing until in January 1999, the CBS/NYT poll reported 55 percent expressing a favorable opinion while 20 percent said they were unfavorable, a high point in her popularity according to these pollsters' ratings. In the Gallup polls, by the end of 1998, Hillary had once again achieved the same high level of favorability that she had during the "honeymoon" days of the first inauguration: 67 percent once more expressed a favorable opinion of her (while 31 percent were unfavorable).

Not only had she regained her popularity in these later years, but a Pew Research Center for the People & the Press poll in 1998 showed her to be "the most popular national political figure in the country. . . ." It found that 58 percent of registered voters had a favorable opinion of her, while 36 percent had an unfavorable opinion. That compared with ratings of 53–38 percent for Vice President Gore, 52–44 percent for President Clinton, 41–49 for House Speaker Newt Gingrich, R–GA., and 30–27 for Senate Majority Leader Trent Lott, R–MS."

Her comeback was quite remarkable. It was triggered at least in part by her response to the sexual scandal surrounding the president and Monica Lewinsky. Her demeanor during this period captured the sympathy and support of the public. Her image as the wronged wife staying in her marriage, however, was quite contrary to the image of the independent, professional achiever role she had adopted as first lady. Figures 4.1 and 4.2 show that as she turned politician on her own, campaigning "unofficially" for the U.S. Senate in New York in mid–1999, her favorable ratings started to decline and her negative ratings increased.

RATING HILLARY RODHAM CLINTON'S JOB AS FIRST LADY

A series of poll questions have asked people to rate the job she was doing as first lady rather than their favorable or unfavorable opinion of her (Figure 4.3).[2] This trend line shows that while approval declined slightly

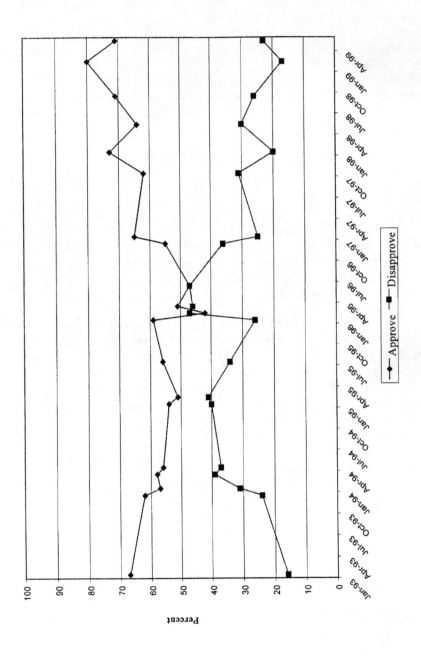

Fig. 4.3. Approval Ratings for Hillary Rodham Clinton.

over the course of the first two years of the administration, disapproval rat-ings climbed approximately 20 points as the percentage of people without an opinion decreased. Hillary Clinton came into sharper focus during this period. During 1995, she gradually recovered her fairly high job approval rating which then plummeted in January 1996 as she was forced to testify before the grand jury. In 1997, she was successful in reestablishing high approval ratings and moderating negative responses for the job she was doing as first lady which have been sustained.

COMPARATIVE ANALYSIS OF THE PRESIDENT AND FIRST LADY

The relationship between how one views a presidential spouse and one's impression of the president or presidential candidate has become of inter-est to presidential scholars and public opinion researchers.[3] This interest is a result of the belief that presidential spouses are a force in campaigns and administrations. Hillary's challenge to the traditional stereotype of the first lady has stimulated this research agenda. There are two aspects to this line of inquiry: the nature of the linkage between presidential affect and affect for the first lady, and the impact the presidential spouse has on assessments of the president (or would-be president) especially during elections. (The latter topic is explained in Chapter 6.)

An apolitical first lady who stresses the traditional homemaker and cer-emonial hostess role may achieve an image independent of that of the pres-ident (or lack much of an image at all.) Barbara Bush, for example, achieved high favorability ratings at the end of the Bush administration while George was going down to defeat for re-election. She hadn't given the public much to compel an unfavorable response in opinion polls. An activist first lady, on the other hand, can create a response quite separate from that generated by her husband's performance. Distinct criteria can characterize public response to her based on ideas of gender correctness, governmental position and personality. Both spouses also can garner simi-lar ratings but be viewed quite distinctly. Similar ratings do not necessarily mean that the presidential spouse has no independent base of support. She may be viewed positively because her husband is viewed favorably, or because of her own activities and stands, or some mixture of the two. It may be impossible to separate out in a quantitative analysis of public opin-ion polls how dependent a wife's rating is on the president's, or vice-versa, the extent to which her activities contribute to positive approval of the job he is doing.

Favorable impressions of Bill and Hillary Clinton closely track in Gallup polls (Figure 4.4). They rise and fall together in 1993 and 1994. Then Hillary Clinton loses favor relative to Bill Clinton in August 1995, climbs back to parity in the October 1997 poll in which she obtains a favorable

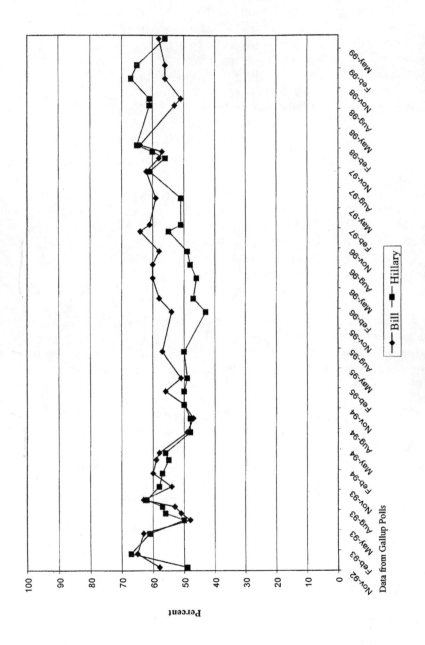

Data from Gallup Polls

Fig. 4.4. Bill and Hillary's Favorabiltiy Ratings.

rating of 61 percent and he achieves 62 percent. The average of three Gallup polls taken in January 1998 as the Lewinsky scandal begins to unfold shows the first lady gaining greater favor while the president's favorability starts to shrink. In those January 1998 polls, Hillary Clinton had an average favorability rating of 61 percent compared to 56 percent for Bill Clinton. At the end of 1998, 67 percent said they had a favorable opinion of Hillary compared with Bill's 56 percent. In mid 1999, as media coverage focused on Hillary's run for the U.S. Senate in New York and her image became one of a politician, her favorable rating fell somewhat and she and the president converged in public impressions.

Chapter 3 examined the public's perspective on Bill and Hillary Clinton using the thermometer scores from the American National Election Study (ANES). Scores were also obtained in each of the subsequent national elections of the Clinton years—1994, 1996, and 1998. Table 4.1 shows the mean ratings for both Clintons for three elections and repeats the mean score for 1992 for comparative purposes. In the elections of 1992, 1994 and 1996, Bill Clinton obtained a warmer rating than Hillary Clinton did. Both are viewed more warmly than coldly based on their mean scores in 1992 and 1996. Both scores fell in 1994. However, Hillary's thermometer rating dropped more sharply than Bill's and fell into the cold range (i.e., below 50 points). Here is a poignant indicator of the toll the Whitewater scandal and her inability, along with the rest of the administration, to produce any health care reform took on people's feelings toward her. A positive reversal occurred in 1998 supporting the findings of the Figures 4.1 and 4.2. Hillary Clinton obtained a mean thermometer rating of 62, higher than either she or the president had scored in earlier elections and she surpassed Bill Clinton (perhaps not too surprisingly). Their thermometer ratings in the ANES are highly correlated. In 1992 the correlation was .70, in 1994, .78, in 1996 it was .82, and in 1998 it was .86 indicating that the higher the score for one spouse, the higher the score tended to be for the other spouse.

Table 4.1. Mean Feeling Thermometer Ratings (ANES): 1992, 1994, 1996, 1998

	1992		1994		1996		1998	
	B.C.	H.C.	B.C.	H.C.	B.C.	H.C.	B.C.	H.C.
Mean score	56.1	54.6	54.3	47.8	58.8	52.37	58.9	62.2
Stand Dev	24.4	21.8	28.2	30.7	29.6	29.9	29.2	29.2

THE FIRST LADY'S POPULARITY IN THE CLINTON PRESIDENCY

Hillary Rodham Clinton's favorability ratings in the national polls, her approval ratings as first lady, and her thermometer scores in the ANES together allow us to construct a summary picture of her relationship to the public as she progressed through her tenure as first lady. Hillary Clinton challenged stereotypical ideas of what the first lady's role should be and thus challenged traditional public opinion about the presidential spouse. She also showed sensitivity to public opinion by attempting during the first year not just to be an overt policy advisor and initiator but to publicly perform traditional hostess activities of the first ladyship. She also lowered her public profile when things started to go wrong and sought to find other ways to achieve prominence, again responding to perceptions about her among the public. A clear interaction emerges between opinion and performance.

It is challenging to feminists that her popularity was restored by her not speaking out against her husband when he so badly abused her with his scandalous behavior with other women and public lying about it in 1998. But she was seen as acting in a dignified manner and that gave her a base of support that she used to become a key figure in the 1998 election. She generated momentum for her being a political leader in her own right at the end of the Clinton presidency. She emerged not as an icon of "true womanhood" but a political force, the most popular Democrat on the campaign trail in that election.

The public was supportive of her initial efforts to play a leadership role in a major policy area, contrary to what our gender biases would have suspected and many in the media have led us to believe. That she was then demonized, but subsequently put "on a pedestal" suggests a greater complexity to public ideas about women's leadership than originally envisioned when she became first lady. Her relationship with the public is a fascinating mixture of public and private roles and complex reactions to her mixing these domains in her tenure.

From a gender analysis perspective it is particularly intriguing to attempt to understand Hillary's rise in popularity during the events of 1998 and how she used the sympathy she gained from that painful experience to become the foremost campaigner for Democratic candidates in that year's elections. Stephen Hess, a senior political analyst at the Brookings Institution has well captured the puzzle involved here. "This is especially fascinating because her current popularity is based on her being a wronged woman, and that is a very non-feminist place for her to be. She is building a new reputation by filling the gap in the campaign that should belong to the president" (Dobbin 1998). "She took the role that she once mocked . . . of a one-dimensional spouse standing by her man" (Clines 1998) and then transformed it into an issue-oriented political persona on the campaign trail.

Somehow her silence and continued performance of traditional first lady duties captured the support of the public. Without an in-depth analysis of people's thinking that went into their increasingly favorable impressions, we can only speculate about the roots of her increased popularity. The commentary of journalists who followed her activities in the fall of 1998 provides us with hypotheses about this relationship. Journalists character-ized the public as seeing her as a woman wronged who displayed a stoic dignity in the face of the embarrassment of her husband's humiliating pub-lic admission that he lied about his involvement with Lewinsky. The pub-lic admired "her guts and spunk." In large numbers they expressed empa-thy toward the woman "who has kept private any pain or humiliation she felt from her husband's admission of an extramarital relationship." People appreciated the way she conducted herself in this troubling period. (This summary of journalistic perspectives on the cause of her support is taken from a review of media coverage of Hillary on the campaign trail in the fall of 1998.)

Journalists quoted individuals along the campaign trail as saying, for example, "Hillary is her own woman." "She's marvelous. . . . She has brains and charm. And she handles everything she does with such grace. I think she'd make a good president herself." "You have to give her 100 per-cent for keeping going when he's been messing around. . . ." In a *U.S. News & World Report* survey, 52 percent said they admired her loyalty to the president while 39 percent "questioned her judgement." Fifty-eight percent said she should "stay and try to work it out" while 21 percent believed she "should leave Bill Clinton." Sixty percent thought she was "a good role model for American women today" while 32 percent thought she was "not a good role model." [4] Of course, there were critics of her remaining in the marriage and comments of disappointment in her, but given her populari-ty on the campaign trail it was the support and sympathy she was receiv-ing that got media attention. The fact that she had worked to achieve a national image as a political and policy person earlier in her tenure as first lady allowed her to transform this support for her actions as a supportive wife into being a political force and a legitimate candidate for public office on her own.

GROUP SUPPORT AND OPPOSITION TO THE FIRST LADY

Given the dramatic change Hillary Rodham Clinton has made in our per-ceptions of the role of first lady, one would expect cultural divisions in evaluations of her and what she stands for regarding women in political leadership. We have found a good deal of variation in people's evaluations of her and her actions as reported in public opinion polls over the course of the Clinton administrations. Substantial numbers of the public have felt warm toward her, and a significant minority (sometimes a majority) has not. In addition, levels of support have changed over time. In this section, I examine levels of support among groups of Americans to better under-stand the cultural basis of support and opposition to her.

Some first ladies were viewed as above politics; partisanship had little
effect on their support. People in general felt warm toward them. The public had no reason to substantially oppose them unless it were to project
their opinions of her husband, the president, on to the first lady. However,
we should expect differences between those who identify themselves as
Democrats and those who identify themselves as Republicans in their views
of Hillary Clinton, given her partisan nature and involvement in public policy. But how sharp those differences have been and the nature of political
independents' assessment should be empirically tested. We would also
hypothesize that women would express more positive feelings than men,
especially younger women and women in the work force, and that baby-
boomers would give her the highest ratings. They would identify with her.
Hillary was often the target of conservative talk radio during the 1994
campaign and viewed as a target of disapprobation by "white males" in the
aftermath of that election. In this section, I examine the degree to which
this presumed cultural divide between the sexes and political partisans
emerged in national polls.

That Hillary Clinton would not be viewed as a nonpartisan first lady
admired by the vast majority of Americans was apparent early on as the
Clintons made their run for the White House. Journalists quickly noted
that she was supported more by some groups than others. *USA TODAY*
headlined in March 1992 that she rated highest among women and the
young. However, by November 1992, that same newspaper noted that
"Women and *older* people have the most favorable opinion of Hillary
Clinton." (Emphasis is mine.) Among women most likely to identify with
the first lady designate were easterners, college graduates, and urbanites,
USA TODAY reported. Those least likely to identify with her were mid-
westerners, suburbanites, high school dropouts, and baby boomers.
However, nearly a year later according to the same newspaper, the first lady
was now most popular among the young (Benedetto 1993).

The analysis conducted for the first edition of this book showed that
age, education and income seemed to have little effect on one's support for
Hillary Rodham Clinton in her first two years in the White House.
Respondents' sex and their partisanship based on their self-identification as
Democrats, Republicans, or independents were the major correlates of support and opposition. Here I first trace trends in her level of support among
men and women and among the three partisan groups throughout the first
six years of the Clinton presidency and then examine the joint effect of par-
tisanship and sex on levels of support. I use the Gallup polls and the
CBS/NYT polls for these two sets of analyses. I then use the four American
National Election Studies—1992, 1994, 1996, and 1998 to develop a more
complex model of trends in bases of support for and opposition to Hillary
Rodham Clinton.

Sex and Support.

The gender gap in support has been quite consistent and quite strong through the Clinton years. Women have consistently been more favorably disposed toward Hillary than men. At the beginning of the administration, men and women were equally supportive, but men's positive impressions quickly began to decline while women maintained their level of support. It may not be surprising to find that women were more supportive of Hillary than men, but it is important to ask why this divergence has occurred. If men were stronger believers in traditional roles for women, this greater traditionalism could account for their lower levels of support. Perhaps it could be that men are more conservative on public policy issues, and therefore their greater negativity toward the first lady stems for her policy stances, not necessarily her involvement in policy per se.

In January 1993, 69 percent of women and 63 percent of men approved the way Hillary Clinton was handling her job as first lady according to the Gallup Poll (Figure 4.5). In April, 67 percent of women and 54 percent of men had an favorable opinion; in June, 60 percent of women but only 40 percent of men said they had a favorable opinion of her—a 9 point drop for women but a 25 point decline among men during this six-month period. An especially large gap had emerged in the early months of 1994 as women maintained a quite high level of support while less than half of the men were supportive. Men by this time were as likely to have an unfavorable impression as a favorable one, while women were twice as likely to be favorably impressed as unfavorably impressed. Both men and women had slightly lower positive ratings in the first half of 1996. After that period favorable impressions of both sexes began to climb slowly. By October 1998, 57 percent of men and 63 percent of women expressed a favorable opinion of Hillary Rodham Clinton. The CBS/NYT polls (Figure 4.6) show a fairly similar trend for men and women although smaller percentages expressed favorable ratings throughout her tenure.

The 1992 election was, among other things, about the "year of the woman in American politics" as women made substantial gains in their numbers in national office. The 1994 election, on the other hand in contrast, became known as the revenge of "angry white men." Hillary Rodham Clinton was perceived to be a focus of that anger and data from the ANES feeling thermometer rating for Hillary in 1994 provides some empirical confirmation of this perception. The mean rating for white males on the ANES thermometer scale in 1994 was 40 degrees for the first lady compared with 53 degrees for all other demographic groups combined. Further, 22 percent of white males rated Hillary at zero degrees on the thermometer scale compared with 12 percent of all other groups. The "anger" seemed to be there still in 1996. The mean score in that election was 43

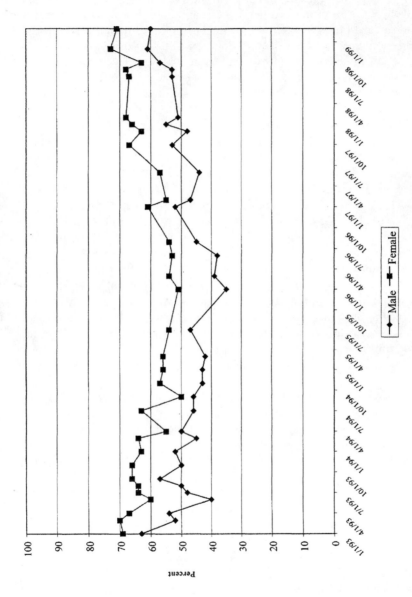

Fig. 4.5. Hillary Rodham Clinton's Favorability Impressions by Sex, Gallup Poll.

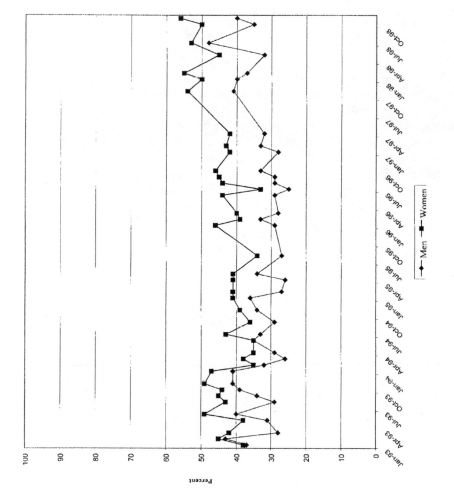

Fig. 4.6. Hillary Rodham Clinton's Favorability Impressions by Sex, NYT/CBS Polls.

degrees for white men compared with 59 degrees for all other respondents. Eighteen percent of white men gave her a score of zero compared with nine percent of all others. As we might suspect, the "anger" of white men dissipated in 1998. The average thermometer score for white men in that election was 56 degrees compared with 67 degrees for all others as a group. Ten percent of white men and five percent of all others gave her a zero.

Partisanship and Support.

Figures 4.7 and 4.8 show the responses of partisans to inquiries about their impressions of Hillary Rodham Clinton during her tenure as first lady. Overall, as the figures indicate, Democrats were highly approving while Republicans were strongly disapproving with independents consistently taking a middle ground. The level of their approval rises and falls similarly across groups in response to her efforts and challenges to her activities.

In January 1993, Gallup reported 53 percent of Republicans and 81 percent of Democrats approving of Hillary Clinton's handling of the job of first lady, while 64 percent of independents gave her positive marks. By April, Republican support had dropped to 39 percent while Democrats maintained an 83 percent favorable rating, and independent voters' impressions had dropped slightly to 58 percent, according to the Gallup Poll. As the administration proceeded, Democrats remained steadfast in their support while usually less than one-third of Republicans gave her favorable marks. The support of independents, always between that of Democrats and Republicans, declined in the first months of the administration, bounced back and then drifted downward, so that whereas over 60 percent of the independents rated her favorably at the beginning of the administration, their support declined to 50 percent in the second year (Figure 4.7).

In the CBS/NYT polls, Hillary almost consistently received a favorable rating from at least 50 percent of self-identified Democrats, reaching 60 percent at points and even over 70 percent in the fall of 1998 (Figure 4.8). No more than 30 percent of self identified Republicans ever gave her a favorable rating except in the beginning of the administration and in the sympathetic days of fall 1998. As with the Gallup polls, independents fell in between the two partisan groups.

Sex, Partisanship, and Support.

The interaction between sex and party in impressions of the first lady is intriguing (Figure 4.9). For example, in the June 1993 Gallup poll while only 23 percent of Republican men rated Hillary Clinton favorably, 39 percent of Republican women had a favorable opinion. These figures compared with 60 percent of Democratic men and 75 percent of Democratic women. A large gap also existed between the support of independent men

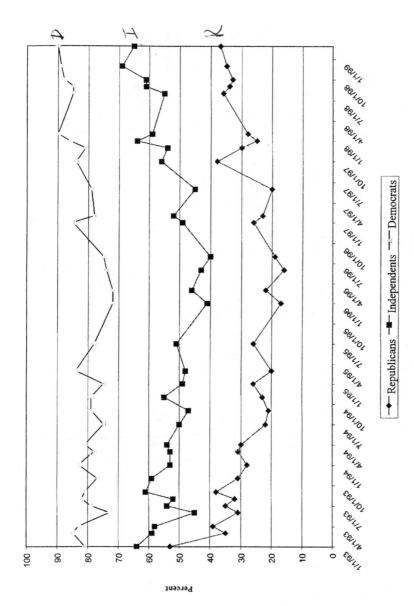

Fig. 4.7. Hillary Rodham Clinton's Favorability Impressions by Party, Gallup Polls.

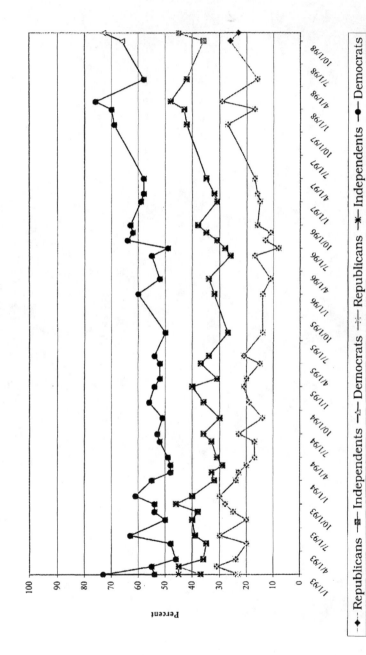

Fig. 4.8. Hillary Rodham Clinton's Favorability Impressions by Party, NYT/CBS Polls.

◆– Republicans ➞ Independents ➞ Democrats ➞ Republicans ✳– Independents ●– Democrats

and independent women. Only 35 percent of the former, but 60 percent of the latter had a favorable opinion in that poll. Early in the first administration, the first lady seemed to be advantaged by the support she received from independent women and her disproportionate support from Republican women relative to Republican men. The gender gap among Republicans was sustained in the second year of the administration. In April 1994, Gallup attributed the continued gender gap in favorability ratings of Hillary "mostly to a gender gap among Republicans: 46 percent of GOP females, compared with 24 percent of GOP males, have a favorable view of Hillary Clinton, a gap of 22 points. Among Democrats, however, there is only a six-point gap: 82 percent of females and 76 percent of males are favorable toward the first lady." These figures suggest a sharp gender gap in support of Hillary Clinton with women considerably more supportive than men, regardless of party identification. Figure 4.9 shows trends in the gender gap in the Gallup polls within partisan groups. (In examining this figure, one should keep in mind that each data point consists of a sample of approximately one thousand people that are then divided into at least six groups for purposes of this analysis. Thus, cell sizes are rather small, with substantial margins of error, making it important to look at overall trend lines and minimize dependence on one particular data point.) While partisanship dampens support for Hillary among some women, it does not totally mitigate the more favorable response she has obtained from women compared with that of men. It suggests a gender consciousness at play above and beyond policy support.

Multivariate Analyses of Support.

How statistically significant are the various sociodemographic relationships described above to assess support for the first lady? I have primarily discussed support among each group separately to this point but have not shown how strong or weak the relationships have been statistically. A statistical analysis of the individual relationships would not be comprehensive because groups can be overlapping. For example, blacks tend to identify with the Democratic Party. Thus, if one finds that blacks and Democrats tend to be favorable toward Hillary Rodham Clinton, we are talking to a degree about the same people. Multivariate statistical techniques aid us in sorting out this problem by allowing one to incorporate multiple variables into the model all at once instead of one at a time, and they tell us the extent to which variation in support is accounted for by these characteristics of respondents in a survey.

Beyond sociodemographic correlates, we should expect that the base of Hillary Rodham Clinton's support would vary among groups with different political philosophies. We would expect that champions of the women's

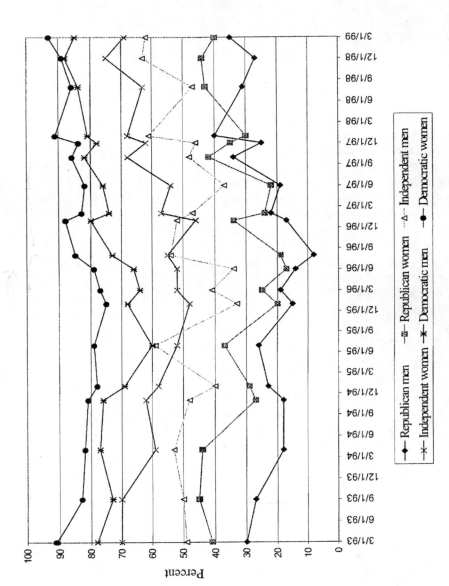

Fig. 4.9. Favorabilty Ratings of Hillary Rodham Clinton by Party and Sex.

rights movement would be among her strong supporters while those advocating more conservative and traditional values would be less enthusiastic about her active role as first lady. Here I combine both sociodemographic and attitudinal variables into one set of analyses to explore their relative explanatory power regarding feelings toward Hillary Clinton. The ANES provides us with the most complete range of questions through which to examine this model. It also allows us to examine over time changes in her base of support by comparing the strength of relationships during each of the election phases of the Clinton presidency (Table 4.2).

In this multivariate model, partisanship is the major force underlying feelings toward Hillary Clinton in all three of the elections. Not too surprisingly feelings toward the women's movement are also particularly related to feelings of support. The demographic variables of age, education and income have little predictive power. Black respondents express more positive feelings than whites and women are more supportive than men. Hillary also benefits from positive feelings about the state of the national economy, but how respondents were progressing economically themselves had little relation to their feelings about the first lady in any of the elections. Moral behavior emanating from the president's sexual scandal was an issue in the 1998 and economic concerns given the robust economy was not such a major issue given the robust economy. Thus, we find that in 1998, unlike earlier elections, support for adjusting moral behavior was positively related to feelings toward Hillary.

For men, the health care issue was a factor in their support for Hillary in 1994. The more they opposed a government health insurance plan the more negative they felt toward Hillary. This finding is in keeping with the "angry white male" factor in that election and Hillary and "her" health care plan as a target. It was much less of an issue for women and faded for both sexes in the 1996 election. (The question was not asked in the 1998 election.) Otherwise the bases upon which men and women made their judgments about the first lady were quite similar.

THE POPULARITY OF HILLARY RODHAM CLINTON IN HISTORICAL PERSPECTIVE

How have the public's perceptions of Hillary Clinton compared with perceptions of her predecessors? Before making some concluding remarks about the public's impressions of Hillary as first lady, I provide an historical review of extant national polls on other first ladies. First ladies have tended to be popular. To the extent that we have had public opinion polls to measure how much Americans "like" their first lady, they show a public supportive of these women, even those who have been outspoken and actively engaged in their spouse's administration. The public has been

Table 4.2. Multivariate Analyses of Feeling Thermometer Scores and Sociodemographic and Attitudinal Variables

	1994			1996			1998		
	All	Men	Women	All	Men	Women	All	Men	Women
Partisanship									
Party ID	.32[c]	.30[c]	.33[c]	.37[c]	.37[c]	.37[c]	.41[c]	.40[c]	.42[c]
Demographics									
Age	.04	.02	.05	.03	-.01	.07[a]	.03	.10[a]	-.03
Sex	.10[c]			.09[c]			.12[c]		
Education	.05	.08[a]	.03	.01	-.01	.04	-.01	-.01	-.01
Race	.13[c]	.12[c]	.14[c]	.09	.07[a]	.11[b]	.08	.05	.11[b]
Economics									
Family Income	.01	.02	.00	-.03	-.02	-.04	.00	-.04	.02
State of Economy	-.13[c]	.10[b]	-.16[c]	-.15[c]	-.16[c]	-.15[c]	-.09[b]	-.14[b]	-.05
Job/Standard of Living	-.08[b]	-.08	-.09[a]	-.06[b]	-.06	-.07	-.09[b]	-.07	-.09[b]
R Better/Worse off	-.04	-.06	.00	-.02	-.03	.00	-.06	-.08	-.04
Issues									
Abortion	.04	.03	.06	.06[b]	.06	.06	.06	.09[a]	.04
Taxes/Deficit	-.05	-.08a	-.03	-.04	-.02	-.04	NA	NA	NA
Health Insurance	-.09[b]	-.13[b]	-.05	-.06[b]	-.03	-.08	NA	NA	NA
Values									
Therm-Christian Fund.	-.00	.00	-.02	.01	.06	-.05	.06	.05	.06
Therm-Women's Movement	.23[c]	.24[c]	.22[c]	.25[c]	.28[c]	.23[c]	NA	NA	NA
Adjust Morals	-.06	-.07	-.06	-.02	-.04	-.02	-.16[c]	-.14[b]	-.17[c]
Adjusted R^2	.44	.45	.42	.53	.54	.48	.34	.32	.34

a=p>.05 b=p>.01 c=p>.000

much more likely to be favorably impressed than not with the individuals
who have held this position and to approve of the job they were doing in
more contemporary times.

"Mrs. Roosevelt More Popular Than President, Survey Finds" ran the
headline in *The Washington Post* (Gallup 1939). In what was probably the
first national survey of public opinion of a first lady, the Gallup Poll in
1939 asked a national sample *"Do you approve of the way Mrs. Roosevelt
has conducted herself as "'first lady'"?* Sixty-seven percent said "yes," and
33 percent responded "no." Eighty-one percent of Democrats and 43 percent of Republicans approved. Women were more supportive than men—
73 percent to 62 percent approval. In the same survey, Franklin Roosevelt
received a 58 percent approval rating as president.

After this 1939 inquiry, Gallup did not continue to ask the public about
their opinions of the first lady. Not until Jacqueline Kennedy entered the
White House in 1961 do we find another national rating of the first lady.
In a Gallup Poll of June 1961,[6] Jacqueline Kennedy received a favorable
impression from 59 percent of the public while 13 percent had an unfavorable impression, 6 percent said they had a mixed impression, and 22
percent had no opinion. These are the only national polls available regarding first ladies prior to the Nixon administration. In 1969, after she had
been in the White House for six months, Gallup asked a national sample
"Do you approve or disapprove of the way Mrs. Richard (Pat) Nixon is
handling her role as 'first lady?'" Fifty-four percent of the people said they
approved of the job Pat Nixon was doing as first lady; only 6 percent disapproved, and 40 percent said they had no opinion. Responding to a
Harris Poll in 1971, 55 percent said they had "great deal" of respect for
Mrs. Pat Nixon, wife of the president, 34 percent said they respected her
somewhat, and 9 percent said not at all. (Two percent said they were not
sure.) Given a card with boxes going from the highest position of plus 5 for
a person liked very much to the lowest position of minus 5 for a person disliked very much, 28 percent rated Mrs. (Pat) Nixon at +5. Fourteen percent
rated her at -1 or lower.

With the same rating scheme in 1976, Betty Ford received a +5 from 13
percent of the population, and −1 or lower by 20 percent of the sample. She
was viewed positively by 71 percent of the people while 24 percent had a
negative opinion in the only national poll available from the Ford administration.[7]

No early readings are available on the public's impression of Rosalynn
Carter.[8] In 1979 she obtained a 55 percent favorable and 33 percent unfavorable response from the public,[9] and during the 1980 campaign she
received a 46 percent favorable, and a 9 percent unfavorable rating, while
37 percent said they did not know enough to respond, and eight percent
were undecided.[10]

Nancy Reagan began her sojourn in the White House with a 28 percent favorable rating while 10 percent said they had an unfavorable opinion, 57 percent said they did not know enough about her to have an opinion, and five percent had no opinion, according to a CBS/*New York Times* poll. She became quite popular during her time in the White House, especially after the first year, when she began to respond to the negative press she received for her gifts, table settings, and other such expenses. In November 1981, 51 percent responding to an ABC/*Washington Post* poll said they had a favorable impression of Nancy Reagan; 23 percent were unfavorable, and 26 percent didn't know or had no opinion. Sixty-two percent replied in a Gallup Poll of December 1981, that she "puts too much emphasis on style and elegance during a time of federal budget cuts and economic hardships," while 30 percent said they were "pleased with Nancy Reagan because they feel she has brought more style and elegance to the White House." In the same poll, 61 percent thought she was less sympathetic to the problems of the poor and underprivileged compared to other first ladies, 16 percent thought she was more sympathetic; nine percent volunteered "the same," and 14 percent said that they did not know.

Through most of the rest of the Reagan administration, Nancy Reagan was viewed favorably by over 60 percent of the people, and occasionally the polls reached a 70 percent positive rating. But her popularity declined and by the end of the Reagan administration a bare majority was expressing approval of the first lady. About three in ten said they disapproved of the job Nancy Reagan was doing.

Bush strategists in the 1988 campaign feared that Barbara Bush would be a detriment primarily because "her white hair and wrinkles tended to remind voters of her husband's age" (Campbell 1993, 3). In an NBC October 1988 poll, 48 percent of likely voters said they had a favorable impression of her; 11 percent had an unfavorable impression, and 41 percent said they were unsure.[11] When she entered the White House in January 1989, 34 percent of the public had a favorable opinion, only 3 percent were unfavorable while the remainder were undecided or had not heard enough to give an opinion.[12] After being in the White House for six months, she received an excellent or pretty good job rating from 66 percent of the public, while 28 percent rated her as doing an only fair or poor job.[13] By the 1992 campaign, Barbara Bush was considered a great asset, obtaining an 85 percent favorable rating in an August 1992 poll, while only 9 percent were unfavorable.[14] Seldom did as many as 20 percent of the people view her unfavorably during the Bush administration.

Barbara Bush's ratings with the public were a poll topic at the beginning of the Bush administration and during the campaign of 1992. But during the administration, she was not a subject of national polls. Presumably because of her noncontroversial nature she was not considered a newsworthy item. There was little to dislike about Barbara Bush or to disagree with in her role as first lady. The people's views of her were a poll item throughout the 1992 campaign, however. We can assume that these poll questions were a reaction to the Hillary Clinton phenomenon: they were asked most likely to provide a comparative perspective.

Barbara Bush, based on poll ratings, was the most popular first lady in recent times; Nancy Reagan was the least popular before Hillary Rodham Clinton's tenure in the White House. The public has been much more likely to be favorably impressed than not with first ladies and to approve of the job they were doing. Prior to Hillary Clinton's becoming first lady, the public's views of the person occupying this position were only sporadically solicited; on top of this, opinions were seldom ascertained in the same way across time making it difficult to make comparisons. National pollsters' interest in first ladies as political figures rose and fell dependent on their either stepping outside the hostess role or not behaving in a properly modest fashion. Questions asked about Betty Ford because of her outspokenness illustrate this point. They are listed below.

Let me read you some statements that have been made about Betty Ford. For each, tell me if you tend to agree or disagree.

1. She ought to keep more of her opinions to herself and let her husband take stands on the issues.

Agree	39%
Disagree	52%
Not sure	9%

2. She is brave and courageous, such as when she had her operation for breast cancer and when she said a prayer for a Jewish leader who had just had a heart attack.

Agree	86%
Disagree	5%
Not sure	9%

3. She has stood up firmly for women's rights, and that is good.

Agree	73%
Disagree	14%
Not sure	13%

4. She was wrong to talk about what she would do if her daughter were having an affair.

Agree	42%
Disagree	48%
Not sure	10%

5. She is too active in her husband's political campaign and should stay more behind the scenes.

Agree	23%
Disagree	67%
Not sure	10%

6. Do you tend to agree or disagree with Mrs. Betty Ford when she said . . . she favors passage of the Equal Rights Amendment on women's rights?

Agree	70%
Disagree	15%
Not sure	15%

7. Do you tend to agree or disagree with Mrs. Betty Ford when she said . . . she would not be surprised if her daughter had an affair?

Agree	60%
Disagree	27%
Not sure	13%

8. Do you tend to agree or disagree with Mrs. Betty Ford when she said . . . if her daughter were having an affair, she would want to know if the young man were nice or not?

Agree	64%
Disagree	23%
Not sure	13%

* Statements 1–5 are from Harris Survey, July 22–29, 1976; Roper Center Online. Statements 6–8 are from Harris Survey, October 6–13, 1976; Roper Center Online.

CONCLUSION

Popularity is an important element in assessing a president. It is significant, too, for the first lady. The survey data examined to this point suggest that it is possible to transform the first ladyship into a public partnership with the president and receive a positive response from the public. This conclusion is based on poll results from 1993 regarding the public's impressions of Hillary Rodham Clinton. Lack of success in policy achievement by a first lady results in a damaging response to the person in that role who might otherwise have served as a consensual symbol in her spouse's administration. Further, a backlash still attends a woman who steps out of the traditional mold that has been socially constructed for her. This is suggested by the ANES 1994 post-election survey, which found a greater polarization in feelings toward Hillary Clinton than toward Bill Clinton. (Bear in mind that we do not have a pure test of the transformation phenomenon because the Clintons' ethical and legal problems over Whitewater were prominent political issues in 1994. These issues must have affected impressions of them and probably caused public doubt regarding Hillary's policy making role.)

The finding that Hillary Clinton seemed to be successfully combining a politically active first ladyship with the performance of the traditional ceremonial roles of the first lady in the first year of the administration actually has historical precedence. We have seen that the one national scientific poll conducted about Eleanor Roosevelt found her to be quite popular. Betty Ford received strong support among the public when she was outspoken on social issues. Rosalynn Carter won approval by a substantial majority of the people for her trip to South America to consult with heads of state as an emissary for the president. Thus, although the public generally advocate for a more traditional first lady, they tend to applaud those who adopt a more active role as long as they appear to be performing effectively in it.

Poll results suggest a complex response among Americans to a first lady who engages in the policy aspects of the public realm. Pollsters have also provided us with information concerning the redefining of the first ladyship beyond general impressions of Hillary Rodham Clinton in the role. They have sought to measure responses to her specific activities as a presidential advisor. Responses to these questions give us an opportunity to assess public reaction to Hillary's activities as a presidential advisor in greater detail. I turn to this task in Chapter 5.

NOTES

1. Few polls exist which asked the same question about other first ladies at the same point. The only comparison that can be made is with a CBS poll of January 12–15, 1989 in which 34 percent said they had a favorable opinion of Barbara Bush while three percent were unfavorable and 63 percent were either undecided or had not heard enough. These figures compare with the 38 percent positive rating and 10 percent negative rating Hillary received in a CBS/NYT poll in the same time period.

2. Most polls in this series ask about approval of the "job Hillary Clinton is doing as first lady," but an occasional poll has asked about her "handling of her role as first lady." I have combined these two versions together in Figure 3.

3. See for example, Mughan and Burden 1995, 1997; and Tien, Checchio, and Miller 1999.

4. The questions wordings were: "Thinking about Hillary Clinton's response to the current scandals in Washington, do you admire her loyalty to the president (Bill Clinton), or do you question her judgement in defending the president?" "Thinking about Bill Clinton's relationship with Monica Lewinsky, which do you think Hillary Clinton should do? Should she leave Bill Clinton or stay and try to work it out?" and "Would you say that Hillary Rodham Clinton is a good role model for American women today or is she not a good role model?" The questions are from Public Opinion Online, Roper Center, accession numbers 0310098, 0310105, and

0310095.

5. Question wording for Table ANES (Variable numbers are from 1994)

V930 Some people feel the government in Washington should see to it that every person has a job and a good standard of living. Others think the government should just let each person get ahead on his or her own. Where would you place yourself on this scale, or haven't you thought much about this? (7-point scale)

V902 Would you say that you (and your family living here) are better off or worse off financially than you were a year ago?

V908 How about the economy in the country as a whole: would you say that over the past year the nation's economy has gotten better, stayed about the same, or gotten worse?

V1014 There has been some discussion about abortion during recent years. Which one of the opinions on this page best agrees with your view?
1. By law, abortion should never be permitted.
2. The law should permit abortion only in case of rape, incest or when the woman's life is in danger.
3. The law should permit abortion for reasons other than rape, incest, or danger to the woman's life, but only after the need for the abortion has been clearly established.
4. By law, a woman should always be able to obtain an abortion as a matter of personal choice.

V950 There is much concern about the rapid rise in medical and hospital costs. Some people feel there should be a government insurance plan which would cover all medical and hospital expenses for everyone. Others feel that all medical expenses should be paid by individuals, and through private insurance plans like Blue Cross or other company paid plans. Where would you place yourself on this scale, or haven't you thought much about this?

V1030 The world is always changing and we should adjust our view of moral behavior to those changes.

V1219 (1996) Each year the government in Washington has to make decisions about taxes, spending, and the deficit. We'd like to know your opinions about what the government should do about the budget. Do you favor an increase in the federal budget deficit in order to increase spending on domestic programs like Medicare, education, and highways?

In 1998, the thermometer question asked about the religious right.

6. The question asked was "What are your impressions of Jacqueline Kennedy?"

7. Poll taken by Harris and Associates, July 1976. However, the people were queried on a number of occasions about Betty Ford's active support for women's rights.

8. However, in a poll conducted by Pat Caddell after Rosalynn Carter was sent by the president to visit heads of state in South America for the administration, 70 percent of Americans rated her trip as excellent or good (Jensen 1990, 770).

9. Yankelovich, October, 1979.

10. CBS/*New York Times*, October 1980.

11. At the same time, 42 percent said they had a favorable opinion of Kitty Dukakis, 11 percent were unfavorable, and 47 percent were unsure.

12. CBS/*New York Times*, 1989.

13. Harris Poll, July 1989.

14. Gallup Poll, August, 1992.

Chapter 5

The First Lady and Public Policy Making

When the Clintons came into office her polls went up dramatically when she started to work on health care.

Rosalynn Carter, interview

Chapter 4 examined the relationship between the public and an activist first lady by exploring trends in public perspectives toward Hillary Rodham Clinton during the Clinton presidency. This chapter carries the connection between the people and the first lady a step further through an examination of the public's responses to Hillary's policy making role in the White House, especially as head of the Health Care Reform Task Force and implications of those perspectives for involvement of a presidential spouse in a substantive policy role in the administration. It will allow for a consideration of the first lady as part of the presidential advisory system and an evaluation of Hillary Rodham Clinton's transformation of the first ladyship.

THE PRESIDENTIAL ADVISORY SYSTEM AND THE FIRST LADYSHIP

Presidents need assistants to help them perform their duties and responsibilities. The radical growth in the chief executive's staff is one of the more prominent twentieth century developments within the office of the president (Kernell 1989). Not only has the staff grown but also policy making has been centralized in the White House. ". . . rather than delegating policy authority to executive agencies and departments, presidents since FDR have internalized policy expertise so as to exercise greater control over the policy making process. Given the expansive role of the federal government in the post–New Deal era, White House staffers have stepped in to perform integral and influential roles in both presidential policy making and politics" (Tenpas 1997).

Since the Kennedy–Johnson administrations, senior presidential aides have become principal policy advisers (Edwards and Wayne 1990, 175). The establishment of continuing functions within the presidential domain has institutionalized subunits within the White House and the Executive Office of the President (Pfiffner 1994, 92). White House staff dominate the policy-making process within the Executive Branch having achieved supremacy over the cabinet (Hart 1987). "Presidential staff have become powerful because they are functionally an extension of the president himself and because the functions they perform place them in a strategically commanding position relative to other actors in the political process" (Hart 1987, 127).

Members of the White House staff are often people who have worked on the presidential campaign or had staff positions when the president held other offices. They are especially valuable to the president because of their loyalty. For example, "FDR surrounded himself with New York political operatives and his more intellectual 'brain trust'; Jimmy Carter brought several Georgians to the White House with him; and Ronald Reagan initially surrounded himself with fellow Californians . . ." (O'Connor and Sabato 1993, 257). (See also Kellerman (1981) for a discussion of the president's kin.) Women have mainly been absent from this circle of power. Rarely have they served as principal advisors to the president. According to Tenpas, who has examined the presence and positions of women in the White House staff through 1994, "women have made substantial gains in terms of both sheer numbers and seniority. . . . Despite such progress, there nevertheless appears to be a glass ceiling that prevents women from obtaining access to the president's inner circle. Thus, although the gender gap within the White House has narrowed, at the most senior level women remain on the periphery, much as they do in the private sector. . . . Whereas women may have obtained the most senior titles and a greater degree of access to the president, they are rarely as influential as their male counterparts who possess similar titles" (1997, 92–93, 95).

Often the first lady has been the only woman close to the president in an advisory capacity. Many first ladies acted as political and policy advisors to their husbands behind-the-scenes, but while in public they preserved the facade of a traditional domestic "helpmate," appearing to be mainly concerned with being the nation's hostess. Those who have been more visible in their advising have met with a great deal of criticism, most notably first ladies Abigail Adams, Edith Wilson, Eleanor Roosevelt, and Rosalynn Carter. Hillary Rodham Clinton has encountered that same tradition.

In *Presidential Leadership: Politics and Policy Making*, Edwards and

Wayne provide an illustration of the principal structural units of the contemporary White House. At the top of their figure are three units. The president is in the center and to either side is the vice president and his staff and the first lady and her staff (1990, 179 and 1994, 186). Pfiffner in *The Modern Presidency* (1994) presents a figure descriptive of the "Ring of Power" in the White House Office which includes the first lady and her office along with the president and the vice president in the top tier of rings (94). These figures suggest that the first lady occupies a structurally significant position in the White House. Also, White House organizational charts since the Carter administration have included the Office of First Lady. Yet few presidential texts have considered or discussed the first lady and her office as part of the presidential advisory system. This background places Hillary Rodham Clinton's attempt to transform the first ladyship into an official advisory position in the White House staff in an historical context.

PREADMINISTRATION

In a February 1992 national poll, Yankelovich and Associates asked "From what you know of Hillary Clinton, do you think she has what it takes to be president of the United States, or don't you think so?" At that point, 19 percent of the people responded affirmatively, while 40 percent were negative and 41 percent were unsure. The important point here is not so much the poll results but the fact that a major pollster thought to ask such a question, particularly at that early stage of the election. It shows the immediate impact Hillary Rodham Clinton had on the national electoral scene as a public political leader, her emergence as a symbol of the changes the women's movement had wrought, and previews attention to her as a policy maker in the Clinton White House.

Numerous polls have addressed concerns about her political and policy-making role in the White House and as a politician in her own right. They provide us with a wealth of public opinion data on a number of aspects of her first ladyship in addition to her popularity. These polls allow for a broader analysis of reactions to her in this position and public acceptance of a more substantive role for the first lady. They provide us with empirical data to parallel a philosophical discussion of gender in the presidential advisory system. An important question is why is it a matter of controversy that a spouse may want to be part of the administration?

Hillary had been the president's political and policy advisor during his tenure as governor of Arkansas. Her involvement in that administration had not been of the private behind-the-scenes variety often characteristic of political wives, rather she had served as a visible political partner. It would have been out of character for her to adopt any other role as first lady of the nation. Indeed, given her credentials, political observers have noted that had she not been the wife of the president, she would have qualified as an appointee to a position in another Democratic administration. (See, e.g., Beck 1992; Clift and Miller 1992.) Hillary Rodham Clinton brought to the White House professional credentials as well as personal traits that provided her with a legitimate claim to be a major presidential advisor.

The role she would play in the administration drew major press curiosity after the election. According to David Broder in a November 1992 *Washington Post* editorial, "Of all the transition events since Bill Clinton won the presidency, none has occasioned more comment than the presence of future first lady Hillary Clinton throughout the president-elect's first meeting with Democratic congressional leaders" (1992). President-elect Clinton was quite forthright about her role. "We just sort of sit down here around the table and talk. She's part of it," the president-elect said in response to questions about her participation in his meetings with key transition advisors and congressional leaders. "She stayed the whole time, talked a lot. . . . She knew more than we did about some things." At a news conference to announce cabinet appointments, Clinton noted "She advised me on these decisions, as she has on every other decision I've made in the last twenty years" (Ifill 1992b).

During the transition between the election and the inauguration, Hillary Rodham Clinton was one of only five people in the room, along with Vice President Gore, transition chief Warren Christopher, and two aides when the president-elect went over names for top jobs (Clift and Miller 1992). She also participated in the two-day economic conference Clinton held in December prior to his inauguration, although she did not did ask questions or make comments.

Whether she would hold some kind of cabinet status was an item of press speculation. A December 19, 1992, *New York Times* headline ran "Clinton Wants Wife at Cabinet Table" (Ifill 1992), and the *Washington Post* headlined "A Clinton in the Cabinet? Not Officially, but First Lady Will Sit in" (Sherrill 1992). Because of the so-called "Bobby Kennedy" law, she could not be appointed to an official position in the government. The Postal Revenue and Federal Salary Act of 1967 passed in response to President John F. Kennedy's appointment of his brother Bobby to attorney general forbids a public official from appointing, employing, promoting, or advancing a relative in an agency in which he is serving or over which he exercises jurisdiction or control. So although she could not be appointed to a formal paid position, Clinton and his transition team said the future first lady would attend cabinet meetings whenever she wanted (Sherrill 1992).

What was the public perspective in anticipation of her taking on a policy advisory role? To summarize poll results prior to the inauguration, we can say that two-thirds of poll respondents were not worried about Hillary

Clinton having too large of a role in the Clinton administration (Gallup, 11/19/92)and did not see her as having too large of a role in the transition (Clift and Miller 1992). Based on the results of its December 1992 poll, the *Wall Street Journal* concluded that the prospect of Hillary Clinton being an influential White House advisor was "fine by most Americans. By 63 percent to 24 percent, Americans believe Mrs. Clinton has the knowledge and personal characteristics that qualify her to be an advisor to her husband" (Frisby 1992).

But at the same time, the public was sending other messages about the kind of first lady they preferred. People told pollsters they felt that she could be an advisor but should not be appointed to an official position in her husband's administration or sit in on cabinet meetings (Walsh 1993). Given an option, the U.S. public preferred that Hillary Clinton be a traditional first lady, advocate for policies and programs to benefit children and testify before Congress on issues that concern her. Of course, they had few historical examples to draw upon in conceiving of such a role. The following questions from pre-inauguration polls illustrate public perceptions at the time.

Preadministration Polls on Hillary Clinton as Policy Advisor

1. Gallup 4/92: Do you approve or disapprove of Hillary Clinton having a major post in her husband's administration?

Approve	25%
Disapprove	67%
Not sure	8%

2. Gallup 7/92: Do you favor or oppose having a first lady who is involved in the president's policy decisions and the day-to-day operations of the White House staff?

Approve	58%
Oppose	35%
Not sure	7%

3. Gallup 11/10/92: Which worries you more—that Hillary Clinton won't have a large enough role in the Clinton administration or that she will have too large a role, or does neither worry you very much?

Role not large enough	4%
Too large a role	26%
Neither	67%

3. *Newsweek* 11/20/92: Do you think Hillary Clinton is playing too great a role in the transition process?

Not too great	62%
Too great	25%

4. NBC/WSJ 12/15/92: Do you believe that Hillary Clinton has the knowledge and personal characteristics that would qualify her to be an advisor to her husband while he serves as president, or not?

HRC qualified to be advisor	63%
Not qualified	24%
Not sure	13%

5. Would you favor or oppose the appointment of Hillary Clinton to an official position in the Clinton Administration?

Favor appointment	32%
Oppose appointment	59%
Not sure	9%

6. Would you like to see Hillary Clinton play an active role in policy-making in the Clinton administration?

Newsweek 12/28/92	Yes	46%	No	40%
Gallup 1/14/93	Yes	43%	No	53%

7. *Los Angeles Times*, January 19, 1993: Do you think Hillary Clinton should sit in on the president's cabinet meetings, or not?

Should	24%
Should not	68%
Don't know	8%

8. CBS/*New York Times*, January 12, 93: Do you approve or disapprove of Hillary Clinton sitting in on cabinet meetings?

Approve	40%
Disapprove	53%
Don't know	7%

9. *U.S. News & World Report* 1/25/93: Do you favor or oppose these roles for Hillary Clinton?

	Favor	Oppose
Sitting in on cabinet meetings	37%	58%
Being a traditional first lady	70	21
Being an advocate for policies and programs to benefit children	90	7
Being a major advisor on appointments and policy	34	59
Testifying before Congress on issues that concern her	71	22

ADVISOR TO THE PRESIDENT

"'Of course she's in the loop,' says an administration official. 'She is the loop'" (Cooper 1993).

When Hillary Rodham entered the White House, she inherited an established office in the East Wing of the building. An office for the first lady has become part of the organizational structure of the office of the president.[1] This office as an official part of the president's staff is a contemporary phenomenon, but Anthony (1990) and Caroli (1987) trace its beginnings to the presidency of Theodore Roosevelt. According to these two historians, the institutionalization of an office for the first lady within the executive branch was initiated when Edith Roosevelt hired a "social secretary" to handle her official correspondence, the first salaried government employee answering to the first lady as her boss. The duties handled on this side of the White House focused on the social life of the presidency; its staff remained small and was not formally recognized as part of governmental personnel until the more contemporary presidency.

Even Eleanor Roosevelt, for all of her travels and involvement in the public life of the nation, had a staff of only two. "At an annual salary of $35,000 [Malvina Thompson] was the first member of the first lady's staff to be paid as personal secretary, but when she worked on Eleanor's personal business, she was paid by her. A former employee of Edith Wilson, Edith Benham Helm, first volunteered to help Eleanor as a part-time social secretary, and her role quickly evolved into a full-time job" (Anthony 1990, 458). They were "assisted by various White House staffers who worked on temporary assignments" (Caroli 1987, 198). Evidence of the first lady's staff being perceived as a formal part of government personnel did not occur until 1953 at the onset of the Eisenhower administration when the *Congressional Directory* "acknowledged for the first time the distaff side of the Executive Office [by] list[ing] Mary McCaffree, 'Acting Secretary to the President's Wife'" (Caroli 1987, 218).

Jackie Kennedy dramatically expanded the first lady's staff until eventually Letitia Baldrige, her social secretary, reported that she had "forty people working under her in what she referred to as the 'first lady's Secretariat'" (Baldrige 1968). Her staff was divided into four sections: press, calligraphy–protocol–social records department, correspondence, and social files. But only Letitia Baldrige's position was listed under the office of the president in the *Congressional Directory*.

Lady Bird Johnson contributed to the development of the first lady's office by "appointing a larger and better-trained staff than any seen in the East Wing of the White House." Her press section consisted of six full-time employees, and two staff members dealt only with beautification issues. Caroli notes "expertise became as much a mark of the East Wing as the West Wing" under Lady Bird Johnson's tutelage (1987, 242). Activities within her domain "became an extension of the presidential office—purposeful activities which were designed to complement and supplement programs, policies, and legislation emanating from the administration" (Foreman 1971, 101).

Contemporary first ladies established a staff that include press personnel, and policy experts for whatever problem that had become their "issue," in addition to responsibility for the social and symbolic duties of the office. For example, the *Congressional Directory* lists a director of projects for the first lady and a director of community liaison in the Carter administration. Since the Reagan administration, the Office of First Lady has been headed by a chief of staff. During the Clinton administration, the position of chief of staff to the first lady has been elevated to the status of assistant to the president (Tenpas, 1997).

Hillary Rodham Clinton's staff has consisted of between fourteen and sixteen people. The list that follows shows the positions composing the first lady's staff for Clinton, Barbara Bush, Nancy Reagan and Rosalynn Carter. The major difference in positions (actual duties and responsibilities are a separate issue) is between the Reagan office with its calligraphers and graphic artists and the Bush and Clinton offices, which did not list such positions. (The 1999 Congressional Directory lists only four positions in the first lady's office making comparison difficult as she clearly had more staff than that number.)

OFFICE OF THE FIRST LADY—STAFF LISTINGS

Rosalynn Carter

Staff Director for the First Lady
Administrative Assistant to the Staff Director
Research Assistant
Personal Assistant to the First Lady
Personal Security to the First Lady
Administrative Assistant to the First Lady
Press Secretary
Deputy Press Secretary
Assistant Press Secretary
Press Aide
Director of Projects
Assistant to Projects Director
Assistant Director for Community Liaison
Director of Scheduling
Director of Advance
Assistant to Director of Scheduling
Scheduling and Advance Assistant
Assistant to Director of Advance
Social Secretary
Assistant Social Secretary
Assistant to the Social Secretary
Assistant to Social Secretary
Calligrapher (3)

Nancy Reagan

Deputy Assistant to the President
Administrative Assistant
Personal Assistant to First Lady
Press Secretary
Deputy Press Secretary
Executive Assistant
Social Secretary
Assistant Social Secretary
Executive Assistant
Director, Graphics and Calligraphy
Graphics Assistant
Staff Assistant
Calligrapher (2)
Director, Projects & Correspondence
Executive Assistant
Deputy Director, Projects & Correspondence
Staff Assistant
Director, Scheduling of Advance for the First Lady
Deputy Press Secretary for Communications
Secretary
Assistant Chief, Arrangements

Barbara Bush

Deputy Assistant to the President and Chief of Staff to the First Lady
Staff Assistant to the Chief of Staff
Press Secretary
Deputy Press Secretary (2)
Social Secretary
Deputy Social Secretary
Director of Projects
Director of Scheduling
Director of Correspondence
Special Assistant to the First Lady
Director of Advance for the First Lady

Hillary Clinton

Assistant to the President and Chief of Staff to the First Lady
Executive Assistant to the Chief of Staff
Deputy Assistant to the President & Deputy Chief of Staff to the First Lady
Special Assistant and Office Manager
Deputy Assistant to the President and Press Secretary to the First Lady
Deputy Press Deputy (2)
Special Assistant to the First Lady
Special Assistant to the President and Social Secretary to the First Lady

Deputy Social Secretary
Assistant to the Social Secretary
Special Assistant to the Social Secretary
Director, First Lady's Correspondence

The East Wing of the White House where the first lady's office has traditionally been located has been considered the social (and domestic) side of the White House. The president had his office in the West Wing where power quite naturally was considered to be centered. "The first floor of the West Wing is reserved for people with real clout. The Oval Office is here, along with the White House Press Office. So are the offices of the White House chief of staff and the national security advisor. . . . The West Wing is where every presidential appointee longs to be. One would rather have a windowless, unventilated closet on the first floor of the West Wing than a suite in any of the other executive quarters near the White House" (McCarthy 1993).

Upon becoming first lady, Hillary Rodham Clinton immediately symbolized her intention to exercise influence publicly, not privately, by taking an office in the West Wing. Her office is a "small room at the center of the second-floor work space in the West Wing of the White House, surrounded not by social secretaries but by the largely anonymous policy experts who will lay out the new administration's domestic programs" (Perry and Birnbaum 1993).

"Hillary Clinton's new job [as head of the Health Care Task Force] and her new office are a public declaration of the influence she's likely to have on the new administration and is a major change in the status of the presidential wife. In the end, she may be no more influential than Nancy, Rosalynn, or Bess, but she'll be out in the open" (McCarthy 1993). Her staff also set up offices in the executive office building, another switch with the past, while the White House's social secretary and her staff maintained offices in the East Wing. Hillary Rodham Clinton quickly came to be seen by some as a quasi Chief-of-Staff. In their descriptions of the first part of the Clinton administration, Woodward (1994) and Drew (1994) often depicted the first lady as being the one to lead and focus debates about the image and the mission of the administration. She accomplished this influence not by acting behind the scenes but by taking part in White House staff sessions.

Not unexpectedly, the news media were fascinated by questions of Hillary's power and influence in the new administration.[2] In December prior to the inauguration, *Newsweek* focused on "Hillary: Behind the Scenes" (Clift and Miller 1992), and in February 1993, in nearly two inch headlines, it asked "Hillary's Role: The Clinton Administration Is a Team Presidency. How Much Clout Does the New First Lady Have?" (Fineman and Miller 1993). *U.S. News & World Report* reported "Now the First Chief Advocate: How Hillary Clinton Plans a Bold Recasting of the Job Description for a President's Spouse" (Walsh 1993) and in February it wondered about "Co-President Clinton?" (Cooper 1993). *Time* described "The Dynamic Duo" in early January and after chronicling Hillary Rodham Clinton's personal and political career, gushed at the end of the article, "If her life continues to enrich his as much in the White House as it did in the governor's mansion, then the country would be grateful that she drove on to Fayetteville, and will soon be headed up the Capitol steps once again, this time at Bill Clinton's side" (Carlson 1993a).

By mid-June of the first year of the Clinton administration over 100 national newspaper articles and 850 magazine stories had featured Hillary Rodham Clinton in her role as first lady. In that same period in 1981, Nancy Reagan had fewer than 50 newspaper articles and less than 200 magazine stories. Barbara Bush had fewer than 30 newspaper and 100 magazine articles. About 300 of these 950 articles on Hillary Rodham Clinton were editorials, whereas Nancy Reagan and Barbara Bush had been the subject of less than 25 editorials (Stuckey 1993).

Measures of public opinion usually accompanied these media reflections and analyses of the role Hillary was playing and should play as first lady. Pollsters have been particularly intrigued with the public's perception of her power and influence in the administration and with an evaluation of her role as policy advisor. Figure 5.1 traces public opinion regarding her influence in the Clinton administration over the course of the Clinton presidency, and Figure 5.2 shows perceptions of her power. During the first year approximately one-half of the public believed she had the right amount of influence. That declined to approximately one-third during the second year. Only a small minority felt she should have more influence during this period, and the percentage believing she had too much influence increased over time from approximately forty percent to over one-half.[3] Four polls between April 1993 and July 1994 asked the public to evaluate the amount of power they thought Hillary Rodham Clinton had. Approximately one-half consistently thought she had the right amount, while about four in ten thought she had too much power (Figure 5.2).

As the administration got underway, the public was quite split on whether Hillary should be involved in policy making—49 percent said she should not be involved in policy making while 46 percent thought that she should be (Gallup, January 1993). And while in December 1992, the *Wall Street Journal* had proclaimed that Americans were comfortable with Hillary Clinton assuming a major policy advisory role, that newspaper expressed a very different view in January 1993—"Poll Shows America Is Split About Her Involvement in Major Policy Making." When asked "should Hillary Clinton be involved in major policy positions," 47 percent

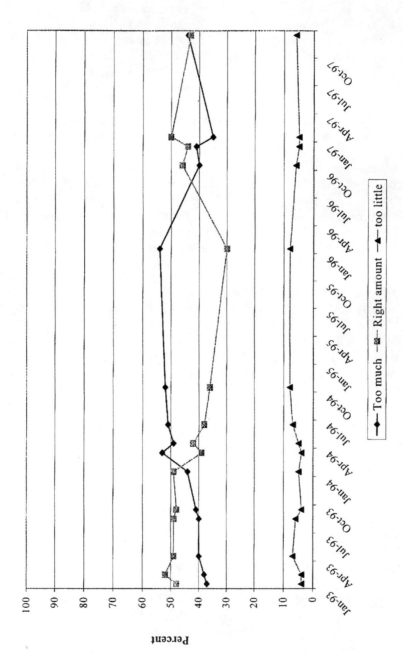

Fig. 5.1. Public Peceptions of Hillary Rodham Clinton's Influence.

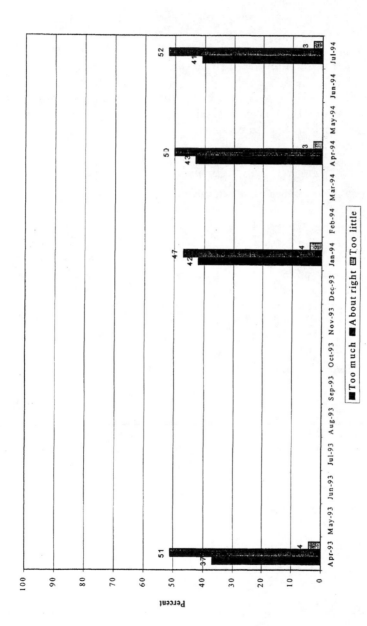

Table 5.2. Do you think Hillary Rodham Clinton as first lady has too much power, about the right amount of power, or too little power?

said yes and 45 percent said no (*Wall Street Journal*/NBC News January poll). *US News & World Report* found people fairly evenly split as to whether Hillary Clinton's playing a major role in advising her husband about appointments and politics would help or hurt his presidency—47 percent said she would help, 40 percent said she would hurt (Walsh 1993). (This question was not addressed in personal terms; some respondents could have been responding to general impressions of how others would view her role.)

Further, Gallup found that after nine months service in the White House, including leadership on the Health Care Task Force, a position in which she primarily received praise (see discussion below), and having obtained an overall positive image as first lady (Chapter 4), absolutely no change had occurred in the percentage of the people who felt she should be actively involved in policy making: nearly one-half (49 percent) at the end of September said she should not be involved in policy making (the same percentage as in January), and 41 percent felt she had too much influence in the Clinton administration. Thus, while they seemed to be quite favorably impressed with Hillary in her role as first lady, the public still seemed to be grappling with the notion of a new type of first lady and the idea of her being a prominent advisor to her husband.

But by the end of the first year and beginning of the second year of the administration, Hillary Rodham Clinton had obtained high approval for the way she was "handling her duties as an advisor to the president" (*Times Mirror,* 12/93). A majority credited her with helping the president rather than hurting him, did not believe he was too dependent on her for policy decisions, and did not believe she had too much power (Walsh, Cooper and Borger 1994).

Thus, at this point in the administration, Hillary seemed to be successfully cultivating public acceptance for the first ladyship as a public policy and political position. Even former President Richard Nixon had changed his mind from his negative reference in the early days of the 1992 campaign. In February 1993 on the *Today Show*, he stated:

> If I wouldn't criticize Bill Clinton I certainly wouldn't take on Hillary, because she is a very intelligent, very strong, very effective first lady. I think it's very appropriate for her to do what she believes is the right thing to do. . . . [A]s far as Hillary Clinton is concerned, with her great abilities, her intelligence and her strong beliefs, she can be a very effective help to her husband, the president, and I think the American people will like that. (As quoted in Jamieson 1995.)

This acceptance of her transformation of the first ladyship is important. But we need to keep in mind that she had also *not* achieved it at the expense of neglecting the traditional hostess role of the first lady. She worked to ensure that the latter aspect of her position received prominent media attention along with her quasi "Chief-of-Staff" and policy-maker roles. (See, e.g., Drew 1994, 101–102). Her first press interview was with the food correspondent of the *New York Times*. The resulting story was accompanied by a front page picture of her in an evening gown checking the place settings for a their first formal dinner. She strived to be successful at both tasks and she seemed to be succeeding. But it did not last.

This acceptance and support faded in 1994 as the Clintons became caught up in accusations surrounding investments in the Whitewater Development in Arkansas and as policy conundrums befell the administration. In the midst of major media attention to the Whitewater affair in the spring of 1994, a majority (53 percent) decided Hillary Rodham Clinton had too much influence as opposed to only 39 percent who felt she had the right amount (Gallup Poll, March 8, 1994), although a majority still maintained that she helped rather than hurt the administration (*Newsweek* poll, 3/1994). Negative opinions about her influence receded slightly by mid-April when 49 percent responded that she had too much influence and 42 percent said she had the right amount. And Gallup reported that "Hillary Clinton Maintains Public Support. . . . In the aftermath of an unprecedented televised press conference, Hillary Rodham Clinton receives strong support from the American public" (Moore and Saad 1994). But as we saw in Chapter 4, her popularity continued on a downward slope after this time. In April, Gallup reported that only 35 percent of the public believed Hillary Clinton is "knowledgeable and experienced and should be actively involved in policy making," while "62 percent believed she "was not elected by the American people and, therefore, should not be actively involved in policy-making," a devastating critique.

Her troubles led pollsters again to query the public about the appropriateness of a first lady undertaking a policy-making role. Fifty-five percent believed it was not appropriate for first ladies to take on specific policy responsibilities in a *Newsweek* poll in March 1994. A similar percentage (56 percent) agreed when CBS repeated the question in December 1994. And Harris found that a near majority (46 percent) believed that Hillary Rodham Clinton's public role in making and promoting administration policies was larger than it should be for the wife of the president, while 31 percent felt it was just right.

The following questions illustrate the public's responses to Hillary as a policy advisor to the president in the crucial first two years in the White House when she attempted to transform the first ladyship into a public policy advisory position in the presidency.

1. Gallup: Which one of the following statements comes closer to your view: Hillary Clinton is knowledgeable and experienced and should be

actively involved in policy making—or—Hillary Clinton was not elected by the American people and should, therefore, not be actively involved in policy making?

	1/29/93	9/29/93	4/22/94
Should be involved	46%	47%	35%
Should not	49	49	62
No opinion	5	3	—

2. NBC News: Do you believe Hillary Clinton should or should not be involved in the development of major policy positions in the Clinton Administration?

	Jan 1993	Mar 1993
Should be involved	47%	48%
Should not be involved	45	45
Not sure	8	7

3. ABC News/*Washington Post* 11/11/93: Just your best guess, would you say that Hillary Clinton has too much influence over (president) Bill Clinton, not enough influence, or what?

Too much	52%
Not enough	10%
About right	33% (vol)
No opinion	5%

4. *Times Mirror*, 12/2/93: Do you approve or disapprove of the way Hillary Clinton is handling her duties as an advisor to the president?

Approve	59%
Disapprove	28%
Don't know/refused	13%

5. *U.S. News* 1/17/94: Do you agree or disagree with the following statements about Bill Clinton? President Clinton depends too much on his wife Hillary when it comes to policy decisions?

Agree strongly	22%
Agree somewhat	14
No difference (vol.)	1
Disagree somewhat	23
Disagree strongly	32
Unsure	9

6. *Newsweek*, March 1994:

a. On balance, do you think Hillary Clinton has helped or hurt Bill Clinton's presidency?

Helped	51%
Hurt	34%
Neither (vol.)	5%
Don't know	10%

b. Do you think it is appropriate for Bill Clinton to appoint Hillary

Clinton to help create specific administration policies, or shouldn't first ladies take on specific policy responsibilities?

Appropriate	37%
Not for first ladies	55%
Don't know	7%

     c. Thinking about Hillary Clinton's public role in making and promoting administration policies, do you think it is . . . about right for the wife of a president, larger than it should be, or smaller than it should be?

About right	31%
Larger	46%
Smaller	11%

    7. Gallup, 3/7/94: Do you think Hillary Clinton's influence has been generally positive, or generally negative on the Clinton administration?

Generally positive	65%
Generally negative	32%
Mixed (vol)	2%
Don't know	2%

    8. Harris, July 1994: Overall, do you think Hillary Rodham Clinton's influence on the president's decisions is very good, somewhat good, somewhat bad, or very bad?

	April 1994	July 1994
Very good	22%	21%
Somewhat good	46	44
Somewhat bad	15	16
Very bad	12	11
Not sure	5	8

    9. CBS, 11/94: Do you think it is appropriate for President Bill Clinton to appoint Hillary Clinton to help create specific administration policies, or shouldn't first ladies take on specific policy responsibilities?

Appropriate	37%
Not for first ladies	56
Don't know	7

    In the second term the issue of Hillary's influence and policy-making role received much less attention from pollsters, but for the most part when queried, the public was much more hesitant about endorsing a policy-making role for her than at the beginning of the first Clinton term. In the transition period to the second term, four different poll questions taken together showed that approximately three out of 10 Americans favored a major policy role for Hillary Rodham Clinton in the second term while six out of 10 opposed such a role.

Princeton Survey Research Associates Poll, October 1996: Would you approve or disapprove of Bill Clinton putting his wife, Hillary, in charge of a major area of government policy in a second term?

Approve	36%
Disapprove	56%
Don't know	8%

Princeton Survey Research Associates Poll, Nov. 1996: What about . . . a major new policy role of Hillary Clinton? Is this something you would like to see Clinton try to do, or not?

Yes, would like to see	30%
No, would not	63%
Don't know	7%

ABC News/*Washington Post* Poll, Jan. 1997: Do you think Hillary Clinton should play a greater role in her husband's second administration, a lesser role, or what?

Greater	24%
Lesser	59%
Same (vol.)	14%

NBC News/*Wall Street Journal* Poll, Jan. 1997: Do you believe Hillary Clinton should or should not be involved in the development of major policy positions in the Clinton administration?

Should be involved	31%
Should not be involved	65%
Not sure	4%

From a research perspective it is unfortunate that the theme of Hillary Clinton's influence and policy-making role failed to receive the attention of survey researchers during and after the 1998 sexual scandal phase of Bill Clinton's presidency. Whether the public's renewed favorable impressions of her during this period were accompanied by a more positive perspective of her playing a major policy role remains unanswered. We could imagine that substantial proportions of respondents might have made a connection between Hillary being a voice of propriety had she been supported as a policy-advisor and played a more prominent role in the White House. On the other hand, the public might not have connected these two aspects of her first ladyship. Americans might have remained skeptical about her assuming a public policy advisory role. The only empirical data available in the form of a poll during this period that addressed this issue was a *Time*/CNN poll, which asked a national sample of respondents, "Hillary Rodham Clinton's role in national policy is more prominent than any other first lady's involvement in policy. Do you think this is appropriate or inappropriate?" Fifty-six percent responded that it was appropriate, while 37 percent said it was inappropriate, and seven percent were unsure. Sixty-three percent of women compared with 48 percent of men thought it was appropriate. Seventy-one percent of Democrats, 56 percent of independents and 41 percent of Republicans thought it was appropriate. And in February 1999, Gallup asked a national sample, "Do you think Hillary Clinton's influence has been generally positive or generally negative on the Clinton Administration?" In response, 80 percent said she had had a positive influence while 16 percent said her influence had been negative.

GROUP SUPPORT FOR A POLICY MAKING ROLE FOR THE FIRST LADY

Multivariate analyses regarding attitudes concerning the first lady's influence and policy making role show the same group support and opposition to Hillary Rodham Clinton's being involved in policy making as was found for her favorability ratings in Chapter 4 (Table 5.1). I use two polls, one from 1993 and one from 1994, to illustrate relationships between group characteristics and support for the first lady as policy advisor. Sex, race and party affiliation primarily distinguish groups in support of the first lady being active in policy making in data from *Time* magazine collected in April 1993. For example, 69 percent of women but only 56 percent of men at that time thought it was appropriate that Hillary Clinton's role in national policy was more prominent than any other first lady's involvement. Seventy-seven percent of Democrats and 65 percent of independents believed it was appropriate compared with only 43 percent of Republicans.

Republicans were both the least supportive and most conflicted. While 54 percent of them thought it was inappropriate for this first lady to have a more prominent role in national policy, 43 percent thought it was appropriate. Forty-one percent of Republicans believed she was having a good influence on the president, while 40 percent thought she was having a bad influence on him. These percentages suggest Republicans were particularly divided on issues of the first lady's influence and involvement in public policy making. That division was primarily a function of differences of opinion between female and male Republicans. Fifty-four percent of the women who identified with the Republican Party believed the more prominent role Hillary was playing in national policy was appropriate compared with only 32 percent of Republican men. Fifty percent of Republican women credited her with having a good influence on Bill Clinton in matters of politics and national affairs compared with 33 percent of male Republicans. Male independents and male Democrats were also less supportive than their female counterparts, but the differences were not as great as among Republican partisans.

As noted earlier, positive perspectives on Hillary Rodham Clinton's involvement in public policy making declined during the second year of the administration. In the April 1994 Gallup Poll, only 35 percent of the respondents supported the idea that she was knowledgeable and experienced and should be actively involved in policy making, and 51 percent believed she had too much influence in the administration. Even close to one-half of the Democrats (45 percent) felt she should not be actively involved in public policy making, although only 27 percent of them believed she had too much influence in the administration. Partisanship and sex continued to separate supporters from nonsupporters much more than other sociodemographic factors (Table 5.1).

Table 5.1. Multivariate Analyses of Group Support for the First Lady's Involvement in Policy Making

Variable	Time, April 1993			Gallup, April 1994	
	Q1	Q2	Q3	Q1	Q2
Sex	.10	.54[c]	.78[c]	.52[c]	.44[c]
Education	.04	−.02	−.02	.19	.20[b]
Age	.03	.01	.07	−.01	−.02
Income	.01	−.04	.01	−.00	.02
Race	.04	.60[c]	1.08[c]	.52	.01
Democrat	.20[c]	.51	.44		
Republican	−.20[c]	−.90[c]	−1.17[c]		
Party				.53[c]	.50[c]

a = p>.01; b = p>.001; c = p>.000

Standardized regression coefficients are reported in *Time* question 1; questions 2 and 3 are logit regression coefficients.

Time questions:

Q1. As you may know, Hillary Rodham Clinton is playing a prominent role in health care policy and other domestic issues in the Clinton administration. How much confidence do you have in her ability to handle those issues— a lot of confidence, only some confidence, or no confidence at all?

Q2. Hillary Rodham Clinton's role in national policy is more prominent than any other first lady's involvement in policy. Do you think this is appropriate or inappropriate?

Q3. Do you think Hillary Rodham Clinton has had a good influence or a bad influence on Bill Clinton in matters of politics and national affairs?

Gallup questions:

Q1. In your opinion, does Hillary Clinton have too much, too little, or the right amount of influence in the Clinton administration?

Q2. Which one of the following statements comes closer to your view? 1. Hillary Clinton is knowledgeable and experienced and should be actively involved in policy-making, or 2. Hillary Clinton was not elected by the

American people and should, therefore, not be actively involved in policy making.

In the Gallup Poll, party is a five point variable running from Republican, independent leaning Republican to Democrat.

HILLARY RODHAM CLINTON AND THE HEALTH CARE TASK FORCE

In the first week of his administration, the president appointed Hillary Rodham Clinton head of his task force on health care reform. Other first ladies, most notably Rosalynn Carter, had had their own public policy projects. But never before had a first lady been put in charge of a major administrative initiative. Public reaction would be crucial to her success and for the institutionalization of a major policy-making role for presidential spouses (if they desired one).

Pollsters quickly moved to gauge public opinion regarding this appointment. They asked whether it was appropriate to appoint her, what difference it would make in actually reforming the health care system, and what kind of a job she was doing. Polls showed early support for her assuming this job. Approximately six out of ten Americans either approved, supported, or thought it was appropriate for the president to name her as head of the Health Care Task Force, while about three in ten either opposed, disapproved, or thought it was inappropriate to have made this appointment. The following questions show how the various polls asked the public what they thought about Hillary's role in health care reform.

1. Gallup, 1/29/93: As you may know, President Clinton has appointed Hillary to head his Task Force on Health Care Reform. In your opinion, is this an appropriate position for a first lady, or not?

Yes	59%
No	37%
Don't know	4%

2. Yankelovich variation (Apr 28 '93)

Appropriate	58%
Inappropriate	38%
Don't know	4%

3. CBS, 2/93:

a. Bill Clinton has named Hillary Clinton to chair his health care commission. Do you think Hillary Clinton is qualified or not qualified to do this job?

Qualified	61%
Not qualified	22%
Don't know	17%

b. Do you think it was appropriate for Bill Clinton to appoint Hillary Clinton to chair his health commission or shouldn't first ladies take on specific policy responsibilities?

Appropriate	59%
Shouldn't take responsibility	33
Don't know	8

4. *Los Angeles Times*, 2/93: Do you approve or disapprove of Clinton's decision to appoint his wife Hillary as head of the Presidential Task Force on Health Care Reform? Do you approve or disapprove strongly or do you approve/disapprove somewhat?

Approve strongly	39%
Approve somewhat	24
Disapprove somewhat	8
Disapprove strongly	23
Don't know	6

5. NBC, 3/93: Do you approve or disapprove of the selection of Hillary Rodham Clinton to head President Clinton's Health Care Task Force?

Approve	54%
Disapprove	37
Not sure	9

6. Market Opinion Research, 2/93: Do you support Hillary Rodham Clinton's appointment to head the Task Force on Health Care Reform?

Support	67%
Oppose	25
Don't know	8

7. *Newsweek*: Do you approve or disapprove of (President) Bill Clinton naming his wife, Hillary, to lead administration efforts to reform the country's health care system?

	Feb 1993	Sept 1993
Approve	61%	56%
Disapprove	32	38

8. National Association of Children's Hospitals and Related Institutions, 1993: As a nationally known attorney and wife of the governor, Hillary Clinton fought for important reforms in Arkansas. Recently there has been a lot of talk about Hillary Clinton heading up the president's Task Force on Health Care Reform. Because of her strong background in working for reform, it is expected that she will work diligently to push the task force toward making recommendations. From what you know, do you favor or oppose Hillary Clinton heading up the Health Care Task Force? And do you feel strongly or not so strongly about that?

Strongly favor	31%	34%
Somewhat favor	44	38
Somewhat oppose	10	11

Strongly oppose	9	11
Don't know	7	7

The public also initially expressed confidence in her ability to handle the job. By the time she appeared to testify before House and Senate committees about the administration's health care plan at the end of September, 60 percent approved of her handling of health care policy, while 29 percent disapproved; 74% said she was doing an excellent or pretty good job.

The headline in Gwen Ifill's special to *The New York Times* on September 22, 1993, ran "Role in Health Expands Hillary Clinton's Power." Ifill declared that:

> Mrs. Clinton is solidifying her position as the power beside, rather than behind, the throne. In doing so, Mrs. Clinton has completed a remarkable public relations transformation, turning the personal qualities that were considered political liabilities in the presidential campaign into political assets now. . . . Mrs. Clinton has no intention of fading away as health care takes center stage, even if anyone were to allow her such a luxury. Mr. Clinton and his advisors have long believed that they have a valuable asset in Mrs. Clinton, and they hope to use the talent for persuasion and politics she has displayed in dealing with members of Congress to keep the outline, if not the specifics, of the health care plan largely intact. . . . no previous first lady has occupied center stage so aggressively or disarmed her critics more effectively. And with each success, her role has been expanded far beyond that of previous presidents' wives.

Ifill went on to cite the latest poll results to support her case. But then support plummeted to 47 percent in early April 1994 (Gallup Poll) after the plan had undergone enormous attacks, and White House attention had been diverted by the Whitewater affair and foreign policy problems. In the same poll, 47 percent expressed disapproval of the way Hillary Clinton was handling health care policy. In July 1994, Harris found a majority still giving the first lady high marks with 54 percent saying she had been doing an excellent or good job, but this represented a substantial drop-off from his earlier findings.

As the health care debate continued to be played out in the 103rd Congress (and ultimately ended in defeat for the Clintons), a majority still felt Hillary Clinton was helping to improve the nation's health care system (55 percent), while 36 percent believed she was "hurting" efforts. The public was also divided on whether putting Hillary Clinton in charge had made health care reform more likely, less likely, or hadn't made any difference— 24 percent said she had made health care reform more likely, 35 percent said less likely, and 38 percent said no difference.

In November 1994, the White House announced that Hillary Rodham

Clinton would no longer head the Health Care Task Force. The president's wife and her task force had created an enormously complex scheme to revamp the health care system in the United States. They had developed much of it in secret, although the first lady had traveled extensively around the country conversing with American citizens as leader of the task force. Secrecy and complexity had worked against the ability of the Clintons to sell the plan.

In November 1994, CBS asked in a national poll, "Do you think having Hillary Clinton chair the health care reform commission was one of the reasons why Congress did not pass health care reform legislation last year, or don't you think so?" The public was quite split on assigning the first lady blame for this failure—43% responded it was one of the reasons, while 49% said it was not one of the reasons. According to Julia Malone (1994), "A majority, 56 percent, say first ladies should not take on policy roles. But most don't blame Hillary Clinton's role for the administration's failure to get health reform through Congress." The following questions show the poll results on assessment of her performance as chair of the Health Care Task Force.

1. *Newsweek*, 2/93: Do you think Hillary Clinton will do a good job coming up with a health care plan, or not?

Yes	62%
No	21

2. *Time*, 5/10/93: How much confidence do you have in Hillary Clinton's ability to handle her role in health care policy and other domestic issues?

A lot	33%
Some	49
None	16

3. Market Opinion Research: Hillary Rodham Clinton heads the Task Force for Health Care Reform. Do you approve or disapprove of her performance?

	Jan. 1993	April 1993
Approve	67%	53%
Disapprove	25	20
Don't know	8	27

4. CBS: Do you think with Hillary Clinton chairing the commission, health care reform is more likely, less likely or won't that make much difference?

	Feb.	March	Aug.
More likely	45%	46%	34%
Less likely	6	7	11
Won't make much difference	40	39	50
DK/NA	9	8	5

5. CNN/*USA TODAY*: Do you approve or disapprove of the way first lady Hillary Clinton is handling health care policy?

	9/12/93	9/28/93	4/22/94
Approve	50%	60%	47%
Disapprove	33	29	47%

6. Harris: How would you rate the job Hillary Rodham Clinton has done in developing and presenting the president's health plan—excellent, pretty good, only fair or poor?

	10/10/93	11/11/93	7/25/94
Excellent	36%	24%	18%
Pretty good	38	44	36
Only fair	17	21	23
Poor	7	9	19

7. CBS, Nov. 94: Do you think having Hillary Clinton chair the health care reform commission was one of the reasons why Congress did not pass health care reform legislation last year (1994), or don't you think so?

One of the reasons	43%
Not one of the reasons	49
Don't know	8

Perhaps the Clinton administration erred in appointing the first lady head of the Health Care Task Force. A number of issues must be addressed in assessing this problem such as Hillary's abilities and credentials as opposed to those of others who might have taken on the task, the political realities of the situation, its implications for the position of first lady, and its effect on Hillary Rodham Clinton as a political leader (as well as on Bill Clinton). While I will discuss this problem, it remains for others more conversant with the intricacies of the political process surrounding the administrative and legislative trip health care reform took to assess some of these issues for a greater understanding of presidential policy making.

Since health care reform was a major priority of the administration and would be a complex process, it was important that the president move fast on the issue and be able to generate a public focus on it. A health care policy expert might have been able to sort through the thorny policy problems surrounding the issue, and a Washington political expert might have been able to deal best with the process of mobilizing support within Washington, that is, getting the votes in Congress for passage. It is unlikely, however, that policy and political expertise would be combined in the same person. According to news accounts, Clinton had considered Vice President Al Gore and Senator Bill Bradley for the job. Gore turned it down, and Bradley felt it was an inappropriate role to assume (Woodward 1994). Clinton was reported to be unhappy prior to the inauguration with what he was hearing from advisors about the possibilities of achieving the type of reform he desired. Thus, to push what he wanted and to get the national focus it needed, he turned to Hillary to lead the effort (Rosenblatt and Chen 1993; Pear 1993). The appointment of his wife would send the message according to the president that "People would know that I was really serious about trying to do this. I thought if we were going to take this on against all the odds, we had to give it our best shot. We had to stretch to the last degree" (Johnson and Broder 1996, 101).

The appointment won initial praise in editorials around the country, and as we have seen, the people were supportive. (See, e.g., the *Miami Herald*, January 24 and the *Hartford Courant*, January 24.) But critics suggested that the appointment was an error because the president would be unable to fire the first lady if she did not produce a successful plan and that there would be no accountability for her actions (Perry and Birnbaum 1993). It has also been suggested that she could have been used differently to generate support for the plan primarily constructed by others. Political debate within the administration was apparently inhibited because she was the head of the task force. Staffers were afraid to challenge the wife of the President. Johnson and Broder quote one member of Congress as noting "the deference paid the first lady by congressional colleagues who he knew believed her to be wrong . . . 'It shows you the way politics really is, that no one's going to tell the president's wife: Ma'am, you don't have any clothes on. Nobody's going to say that'" (1996, 176, 610). This critique of the governmental system is a reflection of the problem of gender in politics.

Health care reform ran into a number of systemic difficulties. The president was unable to focus his legislative effort on it and develop his own political strategy to push it forward, and too many other issues made their way to the front of the his agenda. The Clintons were also weakened by the reemergence of the Whitewater affair in early 1994. Both the president and the first lady needed to maintain a high level of national support for themselves if they were get Congress to focus on and pass this complex piece of legislation. Their plan was also criticized for being too complex, and the process they established for creating and promoting it was not sensitive to the needs of others. Their own mistakes weakened their ability to achieve health care reform. Hillary's suspicion of the press and inability to engage the media became a problem.

Hillary publicly accepted some blame for the demise of the health care proposal. She believed she failed to anticipate the intensity and effectiveness of the opposition and did not realize that the complexity of the administration's original plan could work against it. She also noted her failure to be more open with the press (Clymer 1994). The Clintons can be legitimately criticized for the plan they constructed and the process they chose to attempt to make it law.

The failure even to get a vote on the floor of either house of Congress and the criticism of Hillary Rodham Clinton in the health care plan's demise will make it very unlikely that a first lady will be assigned a similar task in the near future. First ladies will be hesitant to play such a prominent role and will likely revert to private influence. But before the idea of giving the first lady a specific public responsibility in an administration is consigned to the ash bin of history, one first has to evaluate the dire predictions aimed at the gamble President Clinton took in appointing his wife to head the Health Care Task Force. While the first lady was certainly hurt by her failure and her performance can be faulted, responsibility should fall on both Clintons for not being more politically astute as they developed their plan. The media as well as the administration's opponents kept a focus on the Whitewater affair during crucial days of lobbying for the health care plan: a major factor in weakening the Clintons' ability to focus attention on the proposed plan. President Clinton also failed to limit his agenda and make this problem his top priority. That made it difficult for the first lady to carry out her assignment.

If health care reform had passed Congress, the first ladyship would have been transformed. The polls showed that the administration did not have to battle public opinion for the first lady to be able to do her assigned job— the public supported her in this role and had confidence in her ability—and even in the end the public did not seem overwhelmingly opposed to her efforts. She became a target for the political opposition in the 1994 election, with hatred of her even becoming a marketing concept (*New York Times* 1994). This was an added burden on an already reeling administration. She was burned in effigy by tobacco farmers, became a target of the right-wing militia who accused her of being a "doctrinaire Marxist who has recruited 'other American-hating subversives' for key administration posts who communes with the spirit of Eleanor Roosevelt" and has taken the lead in "big government plans to control people's lives." (See Egan 1994; Quindlen 1994b).

THE GOVERNMENTAL STATUS OF THE FIRST LADY

Hillary Rodham Clinton's chairing of the Health Care Reform Task Force not only generated discussion and controversy from the perspective of pubic opinion, it raised questions about the governmental status of the first lady. Critics of an activist first lady have often pointed out that "no one elected her," and thus she had no right to assume a formal advisory position. Yet the position of first lady has assumed some governmental status. Two laws—the White House Personnel Authorization–Employment Act and the Postal Revenue and Federal Salary Act of 1967—and a 1993 judicial decision have created a governmental status for the first lady.

In 1978, Congress passed the White House Personnel Authorization–Employment Act. The main purpose of this law was to curb the appropriation of funds for unauthorized positions in the White House. Prior to passage of this law, Congress had authorized the president to have only six administrative assistants and eight other secretaries. But Congress had routinely appropriated funds for a much larger number of White House personnel without proper legislative authorization for those positions. The 1978 law provided authorization for more White House personnel in line with actual White House staffing.

This law indirectly addressed the governmental status of the first lady. Section 105(e) authorized "assistance and services . . . to be provided to the spouse of the president in connection with assistance provided by such spouse to the president in discharge of the president's duties and responsibilities." Congress may have meant this authorization to focus on the ceremonial duties of the president, as the first lady had long acted as White House hostess, but nothing in the law suggests that limitation. Further, the law was written during the Carter administration in which first lady Rosalynn Carter had been serving in a more formal public advisory role than any other first lady, perhaps with the exception of Eleanor Roosevelt. Rosalynn Carter had stirred controversy by sitting in on cabinet meetings and by serving as the president's ambassador to South American nations. Her actions as the "President's Partner" (Morganthau 1979) suggest that Congress recognized a larger conception of the first lady's role as an assistant to the president in formally acknowledging her status in this law.

As summarized in *Congressional Quarterly Almanac*, the legislative history of this bill made no mention of any particular controversy over the inclusion of authorization for funding of the first lady's office. (Authorization for funding of a staff for the wife of the vice president was also included.) In the debate on the floor of the Senate, it was mentioned that the White House had proposed including the presidential and vice presidential spouses in the authorizations for an increase in staff. In the only mention of this section of the proposed bill in floor debates, Senator Dole noted "'Authorization for the spouse is supposed to be in connection with their official duties,' a committee staffer said. But no one knows where their official duties end. Recently, questions have been raised about the fact that Rosalynn Carter, the president's wife, has at least 17 persons on her staff, none of whom is covered by specific authorization legislation. Similarly, the vice president's wife, Joan Mondale, who is involved in arts programs, has at least four aides paid out of government funds" (Congressional Record 1978, 20901).

Section 105(e) of the White House Personnel Authorization-Employment Act took on legal importance in January 1993, when Hillary Rodham Clinton assumed the position of head of the Health Care Reform

Task Force. The Task Force established a number of working groups. Its own meetings and those of the working groups were held in private and its documents were not made public.

The Association of American Physicians and Surgeons brought suit against the task force to gain access to its meetings and documents. The Association argued that the Health Care Task Force was an advisory committee subject to the Federal Advisory Committee Act (FACA) which had been enacted in 1972 "to control the growth and operation of the 'numerous committees, boards, commissions, councils, and similar groups which have been established to advise officers and agencies in the executive branch of the federal government'" (Association of American Physicians, 1993). The act requires that any committee established to give advice to the president that includes members who are not governmental employees must follow open meeting laws. The law, however, exempts any committee composed wholly of full-time officers or employees of the federal government. In this case, the government argued that the Health Care Task Force was made up solely of government officials and therefore, exempt from FACA. The appellants argued, in contrast, that the task force was subject to FACA because its chair, the first lady, was not an officer or employee of the federal government. The government argued that she was a functional equivalent of a federal employee.

At issue was the definition of an officer or employee of the federal government. FACA provided no definition, thus the appellants argued (and the lower district court had agreed) that the definition of an officer or employee in Title 5 of the U.S. Code applied. According to this section of the U.S. Code, an officer or employee must be, among other things, appointed to the civil service. Hillary Rodham Clinton had not been appointed to the civil service, thus she was not an officer or employee of the federal government. Therefore, the task force did not consist solely of government employees and must comply with the provisions of FACA.[4]

In a June 22, 1993 judgment, the U.S. Court of Appeals for the District of Columbia ruled that the first lady could be viewed as a "de facto officer or employee" of the federal government. The court of appeals determined that Title 1 of the U.S. Code provided "that a federal officer 'includes any person authorized by law to perform the duties of the office.' That definition could cover a situation in which Congress authorizes someone who is not formally an officer (such as the president's spouse) to perform federal duties." The appeals court noted that "Congress itself has recognized that the presidential spouse acts as the functional equivalent of an assistant to the president" by its inclusion of the spouse in the White House Authorization–Employment Act. The Appeals Court stated that Section 105(e) of that act "neither limits the particular kind of 'assistance' rendered to the president, nor circumscribes the types of presidential duties and responsibilities that are to be aided." The court saw "no reason why a president could not use his or her spouse to carry out a task that the president might delegate to one of his White House aides. . . . It is reasonable, therefore, to construe Section 105(e) as treating the presidential spouse as a de facto officer or employee of the federal government. Otherwise, if the president's spouse routinely attended, and participated in, cabinet meetings, he or she would convert an all-government group, established or used by the president, into a FACA advisory committee." The court also noted in reference to the White House Authorization-Employment Act that "It may well be, as appellees argue, that many in Congress had in mind 'ceremonial duties,' but we do not think the presidency can be so easily divided between its substantive political and ceremonial functions."

How can the first lady be a de facto officer or employee of the federal government? The Postal Revenue and Federal Salary Act of 1967 states that "a public official may not appoint, employ, promote [or] advance" a relative in an agency "in which he is serving or over which he exercises jurisdiction or control." According to its legislative history, this is "to prevent a public official from appointing a relative to a . . . position . . . in the agency in which the public official serves or over which he exercises supervision." The law applied to all agencies in the executive, legislative and judicial branches and specifically covered the president and vice president. Thus, the president cannot appoint a spouse to a cabinet position, nor can he appoint a brother, sister, aunt, uncle, cousin, niece, nephew, an in-law, a step relative, or a half brother or half sister.

But a question remains concerning how far this prohibition extends through the executive branch. Does it include boards and commissions? What about service as a presidential assistant in the White House? The court of appeals addressed this issue in its 1993 opinion. It said, "we doubt that Congress intended to include the White House or the executive office of the president" as an executive agency. The court went on to say "The anti–nepotism statute, . . . may well bar appointment only to *paid* positions in government. . . . Thus, even if it would prevent the president from putting his spouse on the federal payroll, it does not preclude his spouse from aiding the president in the performance of his duties."[5] But if, as the court suggested, Congress did not intend to include the White House or the Office of the President in the Postal Revenue and Federal Salary Act of 1967, this should imply that a presidential relative could be paid for his or her service in an advisory capacity in one of these units.

Hillary Rodham Clinton was not paid as head of the Health Care Reform Task Force, nor has she been paid for performing other duties as first lady. According to the anti-nepotism law, it is believed that she cannot be paid. But if, as the appeals court stated, Congress did not intend to include the White House or executive office in the anti-nepotism act, then it should not be illegal to pay presidential spouses for their work as presidential advisors. They cannot be appointed to a cabinet position or oversee an executive agency, but they could serve in the White House in an official advisory capacity and be remunerated for that work. (This interpretation of the court's ruling would affect other presidential relatives as well as the spouse.)

Further, while she seemingly cannot receive a salary, the presidential spouse can hire a paid staff to work for her in the Office of First Lady, and she can serve as an unpaid assistant advising the president on public policy matters. This puts the first lady in a very peculiar position regarding her governmental status. It is especially problematic in contemporary times, when presidential spouses are likely to bring political and professional credentials to the White House which would otherwise make them candidates for top level positions throughout the executive branch as well as in the White House. For example, as mentioned earlier, commentators at the beginning of the Clinton administration noted that in another Democratic administration Hillary Clinton would have been qualified for a presidential appointment. (See, for example, Beck 1992; Clift and Miller 1992). The issue also arose regarding Elizabeth Dole and the potential influence she might have had as first lady had Bob Dole been elected president in 1996. Here was a person who had served in two cabinet positions and other top executive branch positions having to suggest a minimum role for herself as a policy advisor in her husband's administration. The conundrum of gender politics was perhaps most prominent on the campaign trail in that election. Why is it that among all of the individuals surrounding the president and serving him, this one person is singled out for circumscribed involvement in the leadership of the administration?

NOTES

1. White House Office organizational charts which are available for the Carter, Reagan, and Bush administrations include the Office of the First Llady in them. See Heclo and Salamon (1981) for the Carter administration chart and Edwards and Wayne (1985) for the Reagan administration chart. The Bush administration chart was made available by the chief clerk's office in the White House. No organizational chart is available for the Clinton administration.

2. Even the move into an office in the West Wing was the subject of a national poll question. NBC/*Wall Street Journal* asked in January 1993, "The Clinton administration is considering moving the reporters who cover the president out of their work space in the White House. The reason for this move would be to make room for Hillary Clinton and her staff to work in closer proximity to President Clinton. Do you approve or disapprove of this move?" Thirty-nine percent approved and 46 percent disapproved. Seven percent volunteered that it did not matter.

3. An ABC News/*Washington Post* poll in November 1992 suggested that the

people thought she had too much influence. In this poll a majority (52 percent) believed she had too much influence over the president, while one-third thought she had the right amount, and 10 percent felt she did not have enough influence. Question wording is once again an important factor, which can explain the divergent result of this poll compared with those of Gallup and NBC. In this poll, one had to volunteer the response that she had the right amount of influence whereas the others included that response option in the question.

4. Bob Boorstein (who ran the White House communications on health reform) explained to Haynes Johnson and David Broder that had he called it a working group "there never would have been a question about Hillary." The most serious error, he said, was that he 'named it the task force. What a mistake! That got us into all this lawsuit bullshit" (1996, 111).

5. *Association of American Physicians and Surgeons, Inc., et al. v. Hillary Rodham Clinton, et al.*; U.S. Court of Appeals for the District of Columbia Circuit, June 22, 1993.

Chapter 6
The Presidential Spouse as Campaigner

In this and the next chapter I explore two further sets of activities that distinguish Hillary Rodham Clinton's first ladyship—election campaigning and foreign travel. Both of these activities have had an impact on the gender and sexual politics of this position and other women in political leadership in the United States. Chapter 3 examined the impact of Hillary Clinton in the 1992 election campaign. That chapter emphasized an exploration of the phenomenon of a contemporary woman not only playing a central supporting role in her husband's quest for the presidency but being a substantive player herself. This chapter extends that focus by following Hillary's activities in the campaigns of the 1994, 1996, and 1998 elections during her husband's presidency. In keeping with the major theme of this work a key focus is on people's responses to her on the campaign trail. Further, having Elizabeth Dole as her Republican counterpart in the 1996 presidential election provides for broader consideration of the role of wives in contemporary presidential elections. Their contrasting images enhance our opportunity to explore gender issues in presidential politics. The role of these two women in the 1996 election is thus given extended treatment in this chapter.

Hillary Rodham Clinton's campaign involvement is first placed in the framework of the role wives have traditionally played in presidential elections and of women's roles in American politics more generally. The role of wives in presidential campaigns has been determined by the strategic needs of campaigns, conditioned by the larger societal perspectives on women in politics, and affected by the individual personalities of the persons involved.

Historically American political campaigns have been defined by sex far more than other industrialized nations. "Electoral politics in the nineteenth century—an all-male activity—was closely linked with cultural ideas about masculinity. With its rallies, talk, and fraternity, politics then was something akin to sports today. Manhood was frequently an issue" (Stark 1996, 73–74). Mayo and Meringolo describe political campaigning as evolving into "a male ritual in the nineteenth century, combining aspects of religious fervor, work, and entertainment. As the vote was extended to all classes of white men, political activity was a bond that drew together men of great and modest means" (1994, 37). Women were seemingly excluded from this process, although in actuality they found many ways to participate in political campaigns prior to obtaining the vote. "Women regularly supported party politics by sewing banners, cooking food for rallies, and attending political meetings" (Mayo and Meringolo 1994, 37). (See also Dinkin 1995.) Many presidential wives were involved behind the scenes supporting, promoting, and even "managing" their husbands' campaigns. Evidence also exists of presidential candidates' wives playing a more public role than traditionally thought. For example, in the 1856 presidential race, Jessie Fremont, the young wife of Republican nominee John C. Fremont was "so popular with the public at large that many party banners that year carried the words "John and Jessie" or "Fremont and Jessie. . . ." (Dinkin 1995, 46).

Smithsonian curator Edith Mayo describes presidential candidates' wives public campaigning as evolving from that of "hostess and helpmate to formidable political force in the presidential campaign" (Mayo and Meringolo 1994, 37). The "front porch" campaigns that developed in the latter part of the nineteenth century provided candidates' wives with an opportunity to be directly involved in the campaign process. They served as hostesses to visitors in the candidate's home and would then ride alongside their husbands on the whistle-stop train tours that began in the late nineteenth century. Traveling the campaign trail on their own is a more contemporary phenomenon for presidential wives. As in so many other ways, Eleanor Roosevelt was distinctive in her campaign role during FDR's presidency. Among other things, she addressed the Democratic convention in 1940 when it appeared to be in revolt against FDR's choice for vice president. She was also active within the Democratic Party in encouraging women to vote. Lady Bird Johnson in 1964 initiated the idea of a presidential candidate's spouse traveling alone to promote the ticket. Her whistle-stop campaign tour through the South in October 1964 was a significant event. She took this solo trip to build support for her husband in a region that had once been solidly Democratic but because of her husband's stand on civil rights had turned on its fellow native. The *Lady Bird Special,* Mrs. Johnson's campaign train, "rolled south from Alexandria, Virginia, to New Orleans, Louisiana, making stops along the way so that Lady Bird could make speeches and court local politicians. It was a risky but master-fully executed campaign event. She gave forty-seven speeches in four days and sweet-talked five reluctant governors and four senators, dozens of del-egates and several hundred national and international reporters into com-ing aboard" (Hoyt 1996). Polls taken before and after she had visited areas showed the positive impact of her effort (Black 1997).

Since the 1960s, presidential campaigns have become more candidate-centered than party-oriented. The 1960s also saw the rise of the second women's movement. The candidate-centeredness of elections means that the candidates and those around them have come to be more in control of the process and freer to develop strategies and campaign agendas. Their use of surrogates to generate attention to their campaign, raise money, and rally the faithful have become an important aspect of presidential elections. To reach voters, surrogates, especially wives, have become indispensable members of the presidential candidate's supporting cast. Hillary Rodham Clinton's campaign activities should be viewed in this historical context.

How significant activities of a spouse on the campaign trail are is a research question. Statistical analyses of voter decisions in campaigns have assigned little weight to vice presidential candidates and spouses. Rarely have people in these roles been given credit for increasing percentages of the vote obtained by a presidential candidate in quantitative analyses of independent variables affecting the vote. Measuring the quantitative effect of a spouse on campaigns and elections is difficult. Such measurements have sought to determine how important perceptions about the spouse are in voters' final decisions. For example, to what degree would someone who feels indifferent toward the candidates be swung one way because of an "attractive" spouse, or if one otherwise feels negative toward a candidate, might affect toward the spouse be strong enough to swing one's vote?

Two quantitative analyses of the influence of wives on the 1996 presi-dential election conclude that there was a spouse effect on the vote in that election. Mughan and Burden (1997) conclude that Hillary was more influ-ential in shaping the outcome of the presidential election in 1996 than in 1992 even through she was less popular. The 1996 vote analysis of Tien et al showed "that first wives play an important role in the election. First wives, especially Hillary Clinton, had a strong impact on the public popu-larity of their husbands, and they also influenced the vote. The results sug-gest that first wives are important players in national politics" (1999, 165). The conclusions of each of these studies is based on the size of regression coefficients of wives' feeling thermometer scores on the vote for their spouse controlling for other factors considered to be important predictors of the vote. This means that based on a statistical analysis all other things being equal, the more individuals liked the spouse, the more likely they were to vote for the husband.

One cannot conclude from these analyses that wives are a deciding factor in the decision to vote for or against a candidate. We cannot conclude that if it were not for Hillary a certain percentage of the public would not have voted for Bill Clinton. It is more likely that for some voters having Hillary in the White House reinforced their support for Bill Clinton and perhaps made them more certain of their vote, particularly liberal Democrats. (It is also possible that their positive feelings toward her motivated some people to vote who otherwise might not have been stimulated to turn out based on a lukewarm opinion of the president.) At the same time, it is doubtful that many voters said they would have voted for Bill Clinton but did not because of Hillary. Her presence probably strengthened a decision they would have made anyway on partisan and political grounds.

The problem with most quantitative analyses of the impact of the spouse on the vote is that we can only show the strength of the relationship between affect and vote controlling for other factors; we cannot show a causal relationship. But to argue that these correlational analyses do not prove a causal relationship is not to argue that wives have no effect in contemporary elections. Mughan and Burden correctly characterize the importance of wives when they cast their role as shoring up support in particular quarters as opposed to having a more diffuse impact. Hillary had an effect in 1996 because of her popularity in the left wing of the Democratic Party, and she was used to reinforce the support which Bill Clinton had jeopardized by moving to the center. "The trick is less to have them appeal outside their husband's partisan fold and more to have them shore up loyal support within it" (1997, 13).

The effect of the spouse on the campaign trail can be very broad in scope; she can attract crowds, generate positive press, help raise money, appeal to particular groups, and so on. This cannot be captured in a quantitative analysis. Quantitative analyses ignore the ability of a particular campaigner to stimulate workers, raise funds, motivate certain groups, or send get-out-the-vote messages. It is their strategic use within the campaign that has made wives a force in contemporary presidential elections, not their independent quantitative effect on the vote. As UPI White House reporter Helen Thomas has said, "In terms of political capital, the wives of the candidates do count" (1996). Or as Hoyt has asked regarding Hillary Clinton and Elizabeth Doe in 1996, "What if they had stayed home?" (1996) Hillary Rodham Clinton's strategic role (and Elizabeth Dole's in 1996) in the campaigns of her husband's presidency is thus a substantial element in the consideration of the first ladyship.

THE 1994 ELECTION

The 1994 election occurred in the context of the failed Clinton health care reform effort. Thus, the visibility of the role Hillary would play in the Democratic Party's campaign effort in 1994 was an issue. The 1996 election was also played out in the context of an unpopular first lady battered by the Whitewater investigation. The first lady's relationship with the public was markedly different during the 1998 election, however, resulting in her playing a more visible and strategically different role than in the two earlier elections.

The coolness of the public toward Hillary Rodham Clinton during the 1994 election period is well illustrated by the scores respondents gave her on the thermometer ratings of the American National Election Study as shown in Chapter 4. Her average thermometer score was 48 degrees, with anything below 50 points being considered cold in this analysis. Her campaigning for Democratic candidates that year appears to have been rather minimal based on a review of her schedule during the months of September and October. She made two campaign trips to California where she spoke at fundraisers and rallies for gubernatorial candidate Kathleen Brown and for the reelection of Diane Feinstein to the U.S. Senate. She also traveled to Maine, Massachusetts, Connecticut, Michigan and Pennsylvania for gubernatorial, senatorial, and congressional candidates. In addition, she worked Florida on behalf of her brother's candidacy for the U.S. Senate. She also participated in election eve rallies with the president.

Her campaign involvement received little media commentary, suggesting that it was neither extensive nor highly visible. A White House staffer in a Knight–Ridder News Service interview described her very defined role in that election. According to the aide, "She will definitely campaign for those candidates who want her. In many circles, Hillary Clinton is still a huge draw. She generates big money. Some of it is curiosity, but the rest of it is a genuine feeling that she has gotten a raw deal" (Cannon 1994). White House correspondent Helen Thomas described her campaigning that year as being involved in fundraisers where she would "be really preaching to the choir" (CNN News, September 8). The assessment of pollster Mark DiCamillo of the Field Poll in California was that her presence had "a sense of glamour and appeal to certain segments, especially Democratic women" (*Arizona Republic*, September 11, 1994). Given the perception that overall she was a political liability that year, the Democrats used her in a narrow strategic manner to raise money and generate support among the liberal base of the party and attempted to keep her out of the political spotlight.

THE 1998 ELECTION

The context of the 1998 midterm election was very different from 1994 for the first lady as a result of the sexual scandal of the president and her support of him. She basked in renewed popularity and became a formidable force in the Democratic campaign strategy that year. She became "campaigner-in-chief" and a "one-woman campaign machine." She took on an "election-season role that in normal times would have been assumed by Mr. Clinton" (Nagourney 1998). Candidates who were reluctant to appear with the president because of the Lewinsky affair were eager to embrace her. She was the most sought after campaigner because she could "point to the administration's accomplishments without being blamed for the affair that has tarnished her husband" (Pertman 1998).

Media commentary well illustrates the key role she played on the 1998 campaign trail and the strategic place wives can assume. Muriel Dobbin, for example, told us that "First Lady Hillary Rodham Clinton is barnstorming the country in an election year scarred by White House scandal. As a surrogate for a president trapped in the political twilight zone of an impeachment inquiry, the first lady is, in a sense, at last playing *the crucial role for which she was touted when her husband first campaigned for the presidency*" (author's italics). She quoted Republican Party consultant John Deardourff as commenting "She is a true surrogate president now" (1998).

In that election, as part of the Democratic congressional and senate campaign committees' efforts, Hillary offered to attend fundraisers for House and Senate Democratic candidates throughout the country, many of them challengers against incumbents. In June and July she attended six such fundraisers. During the fall campaign she made a twenty-state tour on behalf of Democratic candidates. "Her appearances [were] not genteel occasions to accept a bouquet or cut a ribbon. Rather they [were] hard-charging, bare-knuckle, get-out-the-vote events designed to energize the party faithful, shake loose campaign dollars and win over don't-knows" (Brodie 1998).

She made more than one hundred radio and TV spots for Democratic candidates and raised millions of dollars for Democratic campaigns. EMILY's List, in conjunction with the coordinated campaign of the Democratic National Committee targeted women in key states who tended to vote in presidential elections and then drop out during midterm elections. Hillary Rodham Clinton sent a letter to those women with the theme "children's issues are bigger than politics." She was clearly seen as one who could connect with these women and stimulate them to vote.

Hillary stumped especially hard for Democratic women, particularly embattled senators Barbara Boxer and Carol Mosely-Braun in addition to visiting New York on several occasions to campaign for U.S. House member Charles Schumer against Senator Alfonse D'Amato. She visited Illinois three times, appeared in a thirty-second television ad and wrote a personal fundraising letter that brought in $145,000 in the first ten days. Hillary Rodham Clinton emerged from that election as a potential candidate for national office herself.

THE 1996 PRESIDENTIAL ELECTION

The 1996 presidential election not only allows us the opportunity to gain greater insights on the role of wives in presidential campaigns by following the activities of First Lady Hillary Rodham Clinton, but it also provides a unique opportunity to explore gender issues in contemporary presidential campaigns in greater breadth due to the presence of Elizabeth Dole as her Republican counterpart. Elizabeth Dole had served five presidents, twice as a cabinet secretary. She had even been mentioned as a presidential or vice presidential candidate herself. Just as Hillary Clinton had won supporters who believed she should be the candidate rather than Bill Clinton in the 1992 campaign, reports from the campaign trail in 1996 were sprinkled with similar comments about Elizabeth Dole. Clifford Pugh, for example, reported, "Along the campaign trail, there is talk among some supporters that perhaps the wrong Dole is at the top of the ticket" (1996). One supporter was quoted as saying, as she hopped down from a shed where she had videotaped the rally, "I just wish she was running for president" (Hohler 1996). Commentators, too, sometimes headlined their opinion pieces with the line that Elizabeth Dole should be the presidential candidate. Paul Wieck's piece in the *Albuquerque Journal* titled "GOP Should Substitute Elizabeth Dole for Husband Bob" (1996) illustrates this theme.

But it was as wives that these two women traversed the campaign trail. (In the 2000 election Elizabeth Dole did enter the Republican race for president and Hillary Rodham Clinton sought the Democratic nomination for U.S. Senator in New York.) According to media reports, both the Clinton and Dole campaigns strategized and debated about the roles and activities of Hillary and Elizabeth in that election. Both women traveled extensively and "[b]y design, they move independently of their husbands, tirelessly trying to energize each party's vitally important activist base without diverting the national spotlight from the candidates" (Hohler 1996). But because of the public and political images with which they began the campaign, they were used in different ways, although their roles also converged in certain aspects.

The roles they performed on the campaign trail were tailored to their popularity and credibility, as well as to their husbands' standings in the polls. Because she was seen as carrying substantial political liabilities, Hillary Clinton attempted to avoid the limelight while undertaking an extensive campaigning schedule. She was usually on the road five days of the week although no media traveled with her, and she rarely gave interviews. "As one of the least popular first ladies in history, Mrs. Clinton confines herself to the relative safety of family and education policy issues and, occasionally, to boosting Democratic candidates in regional rallies" (Hohler 1996).

Elizabeth Dole was much more visible and viewed as a key asset of her husband's campaign. She had her own staff of thirty, including a twelve-person advance team to set up events, a travel budget of $1.5 million and a leased fourteen-seat Challenger 600 jet during the campaign. Her entourage was seen as the "first full-time on-the-road operation for a first lady candidate" (Bumiller 1996a). According to media reports and quotes from the Dole campaign, her role in the Republican effort was to maintain a link with the religious right, help carry the South, and lessen the gender gap.

Elizabeth Dole, in particular, took the campaign role of the presidential candidate's spouse to new levels. The media compared her campaign role to that of a presidential running mate. "Seemingly quite popular, [she] does as much heavy lifting as she possibly can in her husband's struggling campaign" (Harden 1996). She was considered Bob Dole's chief surrogate, "one who campaigns six days a week, mostly without Mr. Dole, to raise money and strengthen his support among groups like women and the Christian right" (Bumiller 1996a). It was reported that "Elizabeth Dole at times seems to be featured almost as much as the candidate running for president" although for a period prior to the Republican national convention she kept a "fairly low profile, sticking to traditional first-lady-type of events belying her powerhouse of a political resume." Joint appearances with Bob Dole ended after she upstaged him in an interview on "Larry King Live" in July. According to a *Newsweek* magazine report "After Elizabeth Dole's take-charge performance on 'Larry King Live' last week, campaign aides warned against any future husband-and-wife sit-downs. Bob Dole appeared tentative as Elizabeth finished his sentences, interrupted him when he was on dangerous ground and gently chastised him when he veered off message. 'Joint interviews are risky,' says a Dole adviser. 'Men defer to their wives, and that tends to emasculate the men'" (1996). After the convention, and especially in the last month of the election, she became increasingly visible as she seemed to be the one having a greater positive impact on crowds in the campaign.

The phrase "key asset" repeatedly emerged in media descriptions of how both Dole strategists and admirers on the campaign trail viewed Elizabeth Dole. Among other things, she was a central part of Bob Dole's media campaign, even appearing by herself in advertisements for her husband in eight key states. Further, on the weekend before the election she gave the weekly Republican radio address in which she said President Clinton was not telling the truth about her husband's views on Medicare. That performance was unprecedented not only for first ladies but for a presidential candidate's spouse. Traditionally elected officials of the opposing party served as its representative responding to the president, not an unelected spouse. But no one seemed to challenge her authority to be the spokesperson of the party in a variation of the "who elected her anyway" theme, a charge often leveled at Hillary Rodham Clinton.

Elizabeth Dole also made the rounds of national news programs, appearing alone on "Larry King Live," "Nightline," and "Good Morning America" in the last months of the campaign. In one infamous performance, she appeared on the Tonight Show as a "biker." As the campaign neared its end, "Elizabeth Dole, at times, seem[ed] to be featured almost as much as the candidate running for president" (Pugh 1996).

The first lady's approach to campaigning was quite different. Hillary Rodham Clinton engaged in what one journalist described as "a road show of panel discussions, seminars and workshops before preselected audiences on friendly turf" (Hohler 1996). For instance, in Nashua, New Hampshire, she led a panel discussion with several working mothers and answered questions from an audience of nearly four hundred women. Throughout the campaign, Hillary "kept a relatively low profile, but a very busy schedule, raising money for Democratic candidates and rallying the faithful. Her role was to "build the base. She's doing the party work and the work for women candidates and building the base, and President Clinton is going after the swing. It's a lot like Eleanor and Franklin Roosevelt, where Eleanor built the base and Franklin went and got the swing.' While her husband courts independent voters in Republican-leaning districts, Mrs. Clinton sticks to Democratic strongholds like Lansing, a university town and state capital. And she raises money—millions of dollars for Democratic candidates. She is, by far, the most sought-after surrogate the Clinton team has to offer. In Lansing, her appearance raised about $35,000 for Debbie Stabenow" (Morning Edition, NPR, Oct. 16, 1996). *Newsweek* in September reported that the Democrats had found "a safe niche for her: bringing in campaign cash. . . . She has helped raise $5 million from old-line Democratic constituencies. . . . Democrats filled her fall schedule with at least ten moneymaking stops. Elizabeth Dole may make many women reach for their Kleenex, but Hillary can make them reach for their checkbooks" (Brant 1996).

On the stump, "Hillary Clinton [was] the concerned mom insisting family issues should be above the crass considerations of politics. Her role allow[ed] her to speak to women voters without annoying men and without stepping on the message of her husband" (Harden 1996). Marianne Means (1996) described her as "virtually vanish[ing] as a campaign force.

She travels at the president's side or speaks before friendly audiences about safe topics such as administration efforts to help children and families." Hillary was also nearly invisible in Clinton/Gore advertisements in contrast to Elizabeth's prominent role in Republican ads. She appeared in only one general election Clinton/Gore ad. Hillary was in the background as the president signed a piece of legislation in that ad. She had no speaking role.[1]

National Convention.

Indicative of the complexity and complications of dealing with gender concerns was the question for both campaigns of what role the first lady candidates should play at their respective national conventions. Few presidential wives had addressed their party's national convention. In 1984, Nancy Reagan did lead a tribute to her husband. And in 1992, the Republicans deviated from that tradition by having the spouses of both the vice presidential and presidential candidates give prime time speeches. Marilyn Quayle's speech will be long remember for its stridency and attack upon the Clintons as discussed earlier, while Barbara Bush represented the "gentler," family side of the Republican Party with her more inclusive "grandmotherly" address. Both campaigns in 1996 struggled with what the convention role of the spouse should be. The gender prism was central for the Republicans regarding their considerations of Elizabeth Dole's role. The Democratic problem centered more on Hillary's "negatives" among the public. While they dealt with the issue behind the scene, both campaigns kept telling the press that what the wives would do at the convention was undecided.

On July 24, Steve Goldstein of the Knight–Ridder News Service reported that according to campaign aides, Elizabeth's role at the Republican National Convention was "posing a prickly and potentially counterproductive problem for GOP leaders. One camp wants Mrs. Dole to use her considerable charm in telling Bob's story from the convention podium in prime time. The other camp worries about giving her too large a stage and risking comparisons with 'buy one, get one free' campaign of the Clintons in 1992. They want to use her formidable skills without dimming her husband's star or conjuring a 'co-presidency' image" (1996). In the end, Elizabeth Dole made a major hit in her now famous Oprah-style walk through the convention hall telling Bob Dole's story with the help of key members of the audience strategically placed around the convention hall.

Elizabeth Dole's triumph seemed to have convinced the Democrats that Hillary Clinton would have to have a major speaking role at their convention. At one point Helen Thomas (1996) reported that "President Clinton says no decision has been made on what role his wife Hillary will play at the Democratic National Convention. The decision is highly political and will depend on whether strategists decide to relegate her to a 'hostess' role or to give her the spotlight for a speech." Then at the time of the Republican convention Clinton strategists said that they had made the decision to give Hillary a high-profile convention role, and that Bob Dole's veiled attack on her in his convention speech had "stiffened her resolve" (Fournier 1996b). Her assignment at the Convention became to "try to calm the base over welfare, with women as her particular target" (Drew 1997).

Election Activities.

Ann Grimes has reported that in the 1988 election,

> after their parties' conventions Kitty Dukakis and Barbara Bush both traveled over 50,000 miles. Kitty visited 88 cities in 25 states; Barbara 92 cities in 29 states with her husband and on her own, according to The Washington Post's count two weeks before election day. Kitty gave what her staff estimated were an astronomical 900 TV and print interviews and appeared at 200 events and fund-raisers and at 25 short sessions called "press availabilities" with groups of photographers and reporters. Comparatively, Barbara Bush moved at a slower pace with the media, giving what her staff at the time estimated to be 184 TV and print interviews, 77 appearances at events and fund-raisers and 13 press availabilities. Sixty percent of Barbara Bush's campaign appearances were made with George Bush. In contrast, Kitty spent only 25 percent of her time campaigning at her husband's side" (1990, 144).

Although such a detailed accounting of Elizabeth's and Hillary's travels throughout the 1996 campaign has not been compiled, an examination of their campaign calendars gives us a sense of the extent and focus of their roles. An accounting of their public activities was obtained from each campaign's Internet listing of their daily activities. Hillary's activities cover the period September 16 through October 31, and Elizabeth's activities covers September 6 through 15 and October 1 through 31.

In the six weeks prior to the election, Hillary participated in or attended twenty-seven different tours, discussions, and events. She toured elementary schools, birthing centers, medical centers, and senior citizens' residential complexes. Several of her meetings were listed as "discussion with working women." She attended the unveiling of the Eleanor Roosevelt sculpture in New York and the 25th anniversary rededication ceremony of Disney World's Magic Kingdom. Her activities primarily centered on women and children, education, and health. She also gave at least seventeen addresses to communities, high schools, and universities during this time period. In addition, she also participated in twenty-four fundraisers and Clinton/Gore '96 rallies. She focused on attending rallies and other events designed to encourage more women to get out and vote. In Maine, for example, she helped kick off the Maine Women's Vote Project, an effort to increase voter turnout among Democratic and independent women (Campbell 1996). Women's groups within the Democratic Party had undertaken a major effort in 1996 to reach the women who had turned out to vote in 1992 but stayed home in 1994. Women were thought to be 59 percent of the drop-off voters in 1994.

Elizabeth Dole participated in, toured, or made visits to thirty-one sites during these campaign phases. Attending "women's" breakfasts and luncheons was an oft-listed activity on her calendar of events. She toured and visited schools, hospices, businesses, and a children's home. She visited the Gerald Ford Museum in Grand Rapids, Michigan, and she dropped by a Five and Ten Diner with Senator John McCain in Phoenix. She was listed as giving nine addresses, several of which were given with Senator Dole at the end of the campaign. Usually these were listed as addresses to "citizens" of a community. She participated in forty-one rallies for the Dole/Kemp campaign.[2] In addition, both Hillary Clinton and Elizabeth Dole spent time on bus tours for their campaigns.

The Messages of Hillary Rodham Clinton and Elizabeth Dole.

A traditional role of the candidates' wives has been to testify to the character of the presidential aspirant and to personalize him as a man, a husband, and a father. This was certainly a role that Elizabeth Dole played, highlighted by her national convention address. One of her major messages was to tell people about Bob Dole. According to Dole's press secretary, Nelson Warfield, "She can talk about the man she knows, differently than the man can talk about himself. She can talk about the qualities of kindness and care that she knows from a unique perspective" (La Ganga 1996).

But Elizabeth Dole combined this image-making role with hard-hitting issue messages in her campaign speeches. The extent to which she directly attacked the Clinton administration policies and the issue-oriented nature of her speeches took spousal campaigning to a new level. Her stump speech would hit every major point of Bob Dole's stump speech. She would "[rip] the Clintons at one rally after another, stirring largely conservative crowds to enthusiastic ovations" (Hohler 1996). She even addressed foreign policy issues. ". . . Mrs. Dole's speeches these days are deceptively substantive, touching on everything from the economy to regulatory reform to an areas that even the policy-making Mrs. Clinton has kept away from—foreign policy and defense." She also made a point of speaking to the concerns of women. Near the end of the campaign she gave an address on feminism that it was reported she had long wanted to make.

Hillary Clinton, on the other hand, constrained by her controversial four years in the White House, stuck to traditional themes in her stump speeches and talked in less partisan language. "Hillary Clinton is the concerned mom insisting family issues should be above the crass considerations of politics. Her role allows her to speak to women voters without annoying men and without stepping on the message of her husband. She wage[d] subtler attacks on her Republican rivals in a road show of panel discussions, seminars and workshops . . ." (Hohler 1996). At their national conventions, Elizabeth emphasized the personal while Hillary focused on policy.

The increased strategic importance of spouses in the campaigns is reflected in the PBS' Lehrer Hour's feature on stump speeches in the 1996 election. Not only did the show present examples of the presidential and vice presidential speeches, it also highlighted speeches by Hillary and Elizabeth.

Public Support for the Candidates' Wives.

We know from Chapter 4 that the first months of 1996 were particularly difficult for Hillary Rodham Clinton and that her popularity was at a low point. After her speech at the Democratic national convention at the end of August, *USA TODAY* reported a reversal in her fortunes. Their poll at that time showed "that a majority of Americans now have a favorable opinion of Hillary Clinton, the first time she has gone over the 50% mark in more than a year. At the same time, those having an unfavorable view dropped to a 32-month low" (Benedetto 1996). The Associated Press reported "Hillary Clinton Get[ting] a Post-Convention Bounce" (Shepard 1996). "Polls by CBS and CNN–*USA TODAY*–Gallup found voters' opinions of Clinton had improved a little: 51 percent of registered voters in the CNN–*USA TODAY* poll conducted Wednesday and Thursday, had a favorable opinion of the first lady, up from 47 percent in an August 16–18 poll. The CBS poll found a similar bounce, up 3 percentage points from a week before, although half the interviews were conducted before Clinton gave her speech."

Pollsters also measured the public's favorable and unfavorable impressions of Elizabeth Dole throughout the 1996 campaign season. She tended to be viewed favorably by 45 to 55 percent of respondents. Her negative ratings were usually in the "teens," rising somewhat to about 20 to 25 percent near the end of the campaign. Substantial minorities felt they had not heard enough to have an opinion. It was not so much the case that Elizabeth was more popular than Hillary, but that she had fewer detractors.

Perhaps not unexpectedly, pollsters were interested in comparative perspectives on the two candidates' wives. On at least five occasions they asked the public whom they thought would be better suited to be first lady: Elizabeth Dole or Hillary Clinton. The public was fairly evenly divided in its assessment.[3] In the first two polls, after the Republican national convention where she had been a hit with her Oprah-style address and before the Democratic convention, Elizabeth Dole held a substantial advantage over the sitting first lady. That reverted after the convention's limelight faded.[4] Thus, it would be a mistake to say that Hillary Clinton was a negative in the Clinton campaign relative to Elizabeth Dole; however, we can say that according to the polls she did not have the advantage that a more non-political first lady might have had in such a contest due to being better known. Elizabeth Dole was advantaged in that while she was not particularly more popular than Hillary, she had a much smaller base of people opposed to her. She tended either to be received favorably or not to have made an impression on potential voters.

Table 6.1. Regardless of whom you support for president, from what you know about Hillary Clinton and Elizabeth Dole, which do you think is better suited to be the first lady?

Spouse	Aug. 15	Aug. 20	Aug. 28	Aug. 29	Sept. 4
E. Dole	42%	49%	39%	43%	43%
H. Clinton	28%	32%	41%	42%	39%

Sources:
August 15 poll–Princeton Survey Research
August 20 poll–NBC/*Wall Street Journal*
August 28 poll–Princeton Survey Research
August 29 poll–Gallup
September 4 poll–Yankelovich

CAMPAIGNING WIVES, THE WOMEN'S VOTE, AND FEMINISM

The campaigning of Elizabeth Dole and Hillary Rodham Clinton illustrates a number of concerns regarding cultural issues relevant to feminism and to the evolving role of wives as surrogates on the campaign trail as well as a perspective on contemporary presidential campaigning. Relationships to the traditional role of political wives to speak to women voters, the role of first lady in the presidency, and the strategic importance of spouses in presidential campaigns are three of these concerns.

The Women's Vote.

In her description of the 1988 campaign for the presidency, Ann Grimes (1990) noted that wives were helping to narrow the so-called gender gap. "They could reach out to the ten million female voters who were expected to make the difference in this election. Operatives hoped candidates' wives with their own professions could boost their husbands' images as sympathetic to women's concerns. Working wives of candidates sharing their own juggling acts—kids, job, home, and husband, plus campaign—wives with jobs talking "pocketbook issues," wives talking day care, parental leave, pay equity—would reach at least half of the many two-income couples out there." Using wives to affect the gender gap was a new twist on an older idea of employing wives to connect with women voters. From an historical perspective, we find that when wives began to go out on the campaign trail, one of their major tasks was to encourage women to vote for their husbands. Their appeal was aimed at women voters. A good example, comes from Gil Troy's description of the strategic use of Mamie Eisenhower in the 1956 election. According to Troy,

> Ike insisted that his advisers take advantage of Mamie's popularity. 'Mamie is a wonderful campaigner and, I truly believe, the best vote-getter in the family,' he boasted. The women's Division of Citizens for Eisenhower–Nixon used Mamie's popularity to justify a bigger role for women. Republicans recognized 'the vital importance to this country of her role, and the heart-warming way in which she has filled it.' Deeming Mamie 'the ideal with which every woman can identify herself,' the campaign praised her 'fine' example 'as a wife, mother, grandmother, helpmate, patriotic citizen. And her 'delightful, modest and gracious . . . personality.' Republicans, especially women, were commanded: 'BRAG ABOUT OUR MAMIE!' (1997, 86).

Both Hillary Clinton and Elizabeth Dole were charged with the traditional task of appealing to women voters in the 1996 campaign (Hillary also performed that function in 1998.) GOP strategists saw Elizabeth Dole "as the bridge over the candidate's yawning gender gap" (La Ganga 1996). Her job during the campaign was to help convince women to vote for her husband, as mentioned in numerous news accounts of the Dole strategy. Shaping a candidate's image has been a traditional job of their spouses in campaigns. Giving people a glimpse of Bob Dole "the man" was a major focus of Elizabeth Dole's campaigning. As we can see from Hillary Clinton's activities, she too played a key role in mobilizing women for her husband. Her themes were issues thought to be of particular concern to women, her campaign events focused on women as a group, and much of her energy was spent raising money for women candidates. Thus, at least in one way strategies regarding spouses on the campaign trail in 1996 connected to traditional roles for wives, although in the case of Hillary Rodham Clinton it had a clearer connection to the women's movement and equality for women. However, she did emphasize more traditional issues in her speeches.

The First Ladyship.

The 1996 campaign touched on the complicated issue of what the first ladyship should be about. It had everything to do with gender roles. Hillary's prominent role in the 1992 campaign had initiated this discussion about the first ladyship, and her activities as first lady continued it as a conundrum in the area of public policy-making and equal rights for women. Further, two-career couples that are much a part of the American landscape of the 1990s has forced a rethinking of the traditional way in which the first ladyship has been defined and structured. The issue became particularly complex in 1996 because of the status of Elizabeth Dole with her impressive resume and independent political base. But the Republican campaign felt it necessary to downplay her future role in order to appeal to a culturally conservative constituency and to serve as a contrast to the lighting rod that Hillary Rodham Clinton had been to the political right.

It is not unheard of for first lady candidates to campaign against each other. But the extent to which Elizabeth Dole was promoted as not being Hillary Clinton may have been unprecedented. The Dole campaign searched for ways to emphasize that Elizabeth was *not* Hillary. "The men and women running Bob Dole's presidential campaign are happy to tell people what Elizabeth Dole is not. She is not, they say, Hillary Clinton, and she would not be an unelected policy maker as first lady" (Bumiller 1996a). It was a very tricky case to make given Elizabeth Dole's resume and the necessarily prominent role she was to play in the campaign (as the more attractive of the presidential couple), and the fact that they did not wish to alienate women who might see such a strategy as opposition to political equality for women or at least a put-down of their achievements. She "quickly established herself as a natural campaigner conscious of the delicate balance she must strike as an independent woman and a political spouse" (Bumiller 1996a).

Gender concerns particularly structured how Elizabeth Dole was to be perceived in the campaign. Bob Dole tripped over this concern occasionally, especially as he tried to make the case that she was not Hillary Clinton. In June, he told a crowd in California, " 'When I'm elected, she will not be in charge of health care. Don't worry about it. Or in charge of anything else.' When the crowd fell into an awkward silence at that last remark, Mr. Dole tried to recover. 'I didn't say that,' he said" (Bumiller 1996a). Of course, Elizabeth Dole's contention that she would resume her job as head of the American Red Cross could be viewed as a most dramatic turn away from the whole idea of a first lady consumed by her hostess role in the White House. Had that come to pass it might have contributed to a new perspective on the first lady and enhanced the idea of the presidential spouse being an independent person. But the independent career route for presidential spouses avoids the more difficult question of a presidential spouse being an advisor to the president. That, of course, is what had caused such difficulties for Hillary. It goes directly to the heart of the gender politics puzzle centered on the first ladyship.

Hillary Rodham Clinton's less prominent presence in the campaign was an attempt to lower the level of debate over what role she would play in a second Clinton administration and to keep her from being an issue in the campaign. Thus, both campaigns tried to avoid discussion of a revised first ladyship constructed along the lines of a presidential assistant involved in policy-making and advising, although President Clinton did test the waters slightly by suggesting that in his second administration Hillary might be in charge of health care reform. The extent to which an administrative role for the first lady was a problem on the campaign trail, and the fact that attempts were made to minimize it, reflects the continued gender bias in American politics. This problem limits the opportunities of the presidential spouse and hides her ability to be a political leader. It also contradicts their strategic importance in their spouses' campaigns for the presidency.

Strategic Importance of Wives in Campaigns.

Presidential wives' roles in campaigning have become more extensive, more formal and central, probably with more effort going into strategizing about their activities, statements, and performances in the 1996 election than ever before. This trend has occurred while ironically many argue against a formal role for the first lady in White House policy making and some argue for a greater independence and separation of the presidential spouse, always a wife, from the presidency. Sex roles and gender politics issues continue to frame the campaigning of presidential wives as reflected in the focuses and activities of Hillary Rodham Clinton and Elizabeth Dole in the 1996 election. The expanded and key role wives have come to play in presidential campaigns influences the decision-making process in these elections. Their activities on the campaign trail are a central aspect of contemporary presidential campaigning. Strategizing about their campaign functions because they are the wife and "helpmate" has had a particular cast to it distinctive from other aspects of the campaign. Presidential wives are part of the election team that puts the man in the White House. To be a central part of the campaign organization but then to be constrained regarding involvement in the winning organization once it takes office as part of the White House staff would seem to be unnatural. But that is one of the gender questions that drive this reflection on the first ladyship.

NOTES

1. I want to thank Lynda Lee Kaid for providing me with this information.

2. What are downplayed here are her more private meetings with religious groups. Elizabeth Dole had traveled the country extensively in previous years discussing the "difference Jesus Christ has made in my life."

3. A June 1996 poll in California reached a similar conclusion. Voters in California were evenly divided as to whom they would admire as the country's first lady. Forty-three percent admired Hillary Clinton more as first lady and 41 percent picked Elizabeth Dole. (*The Field Poll*, release #1797, June 1996.)

4. However, a Fox News poll in early October found 47 percent of a national sample of likely voters saying they would rather have Elizabeth Dole as first lady, while 40 percent said they would rather have Hillary Clinton.

Chapter 7

The First Lady, Hillary Rodham Clinton, and International Politics

Our focus to this point has been on domestic politics. The accepted roles of first ladies and their involvement in policy have tended to exclude foreign policy forays and international relations. Exceptions have been occasional goodwill ambassador visits to countries where the United States wishes to be known as a friend but do not enjoy enough strategic importance to warrant a presidential visit. These trips have traditionally been ceremonial ventures without substantive policy implications. A few overseas trips of first ladies have been historical exceptions.

HISTORICAL PRECEDENTS

Eleanor Roosevelt was deeply involved in domestic politics, conducting advocacy on behalf of minorities, women, and laborers.[1] But she also helped in the war effort during World War II involving, among other things, overseas trips. In 1942, she flew to England to visit U.S. troops and energize the British populace. She "inspected bombed London, American Red Cross units, women's training centers and voluntary services, the defense grottoes beneath the white cliffs of Dover, a Spitfire factory. . . . At a shipyard, in the cold drizzle, she addressed fifteen thousand workers. She spoke on the BBC. She lunched with women members of Parliament" (Anthony 1990, 494). In 1943, she flew to the South Pacific to visit the troops stationed there. But when her husband met with Churchill and Stalin in Casablanca, Teheran, and Yalta to discuss war policy and the post-World War II world, the first lady was not allowed to accompany him. Women were not supposed to be a part of such meetings. When Churchill brought his daughter to Teheran, Franklin Roosevelt took his daughter,

Anna, to Yalta, but he still would not let his wife participate in this event (Goodwin 1994).

In time, the first ladies' activities in foreign affairs gradually went beyond being a ceremonial surrogate for the president by representing the United States at weddings, inaugurations, and funerals. In 1972, Pat Nixon became the only first lady to visit and officially represent the president in Africa. She served as the president's personal diplomatic emissary on a trip to Liberia for the inauguration of its president and on a tour of Ghana and the Ivory Coast.

The importance of this trip for our purposes here is that Pat Nixon conferred privately and substantively with the leaders of these nations. Prior to embarking on the trip, the first lady was briefed by Henry Kissinger, then President Nixon's advisor on national security. The State Department prepared talking points for her on issues that included Rhodesian and South African policy and future economic aid, and she received updates on the president's planned trips to Peking and Moscow. She played a political role, reporting back to the president, among other things, that the Ivory Coast president did not believe in using force against South Africa. Presidential assistant Chuck Colson sent a seven-page memo about her trip to the president, stating that "Mrs. Nixon has now broken through where we have failed. . . . People, men—and women—identify with her—and in return with you." (Anthony 1991, 197; also see Robertson 1972.)

This trip was primarily a ceremonial goodwill tour, and its presentation here is not meant to be a revisionist history of the limited role Pat Nixon was allowed to play in her husband's administration. But as *Time* magazine pointed out, it was the first time a first lady had conferred with a head of state on behalf of the president (1972, 12–14). This activity should not be ignored if we are to construct an accurate accounting of the first lady's role in public policy. At the same time, we should note that the foreign relations excursions first ladies have undertaken on behalf of their husbands' administrations have been exclusively to countries not considered in the "first tier" of diplomatic and strategic importance. We might also ask whether U.S. presidents have ever received the spouse of another nation's head of state as an official representative sent with a substantive message and diplomatic discussion points.

Pat Nixon's diplomatic foray produced no negative media reaction. This was not the case in the initial press coverage leading up to Rosalynn Carter's foreign relations trip to confer with the heads of seven Latin American nations in the summer 1977. According to Rosalynn Carter's memoirs, her husband had asked her to go on this mission. In announcing the trip President Carter described his wife as a "'political partner of mine' who would conduct substantive talks with the leaders of those countries and bring back a report on how we might strengthen our ties" (*U.S. News*

& World Report 1977, 36). He noted that she was well versed in policy matters. The press release from the first lady's office said the "visit was on *behalf of the president to express his friendship and good will* and to conduct substantive talks with leaders of those nations on issues of bilateral, regional, and global importance" (emphasis added) (Foreman 1977). Rosalynn Carter pointed out that she would not be conducting negotiations. In articles regarding the prospective trip, both the *New York Times* and *The Washington Post* reported on the "substantive talks" Mrs. Carter planned with government representatives during her visit. Both of these newspapers placed quotation marks around the term *substantive talks*. The *New York Times* continued to refer to the talks in this manner, thus suggesting its skepticism in the days preceding her departure.

The culture of Latin American states was not particularly receptive to a diplomatic mission by the president's wife. Some of the leaders of the countries Rosalynn Carter was to visit expressed displeasure that "Carter would send a woman, particularly one who is not an expert on inter-American affairs, to discuss serious policy issues" (McBee 1977). One Brazilian journalist described the situation as one of being promoted from "the backyard of U.S. foreign policy . . . to the kitchen" (McBee 1977). It was believed she would not be taken seriously.

But Rosalynn Carter spent many hours being briefed for her meetings and taking Spanish lessons. She ended up discussing trade relations, drug trafficking, nuclear proliferation, national security problems, and human rights issues with the heads of state of seven nations. Her meetings often extended longer than initially scheduled, suggesting that the leaders took her seriously. Upon her return, President Carter welcomed her home, "obviously pleased with the results of the trip and with his wife's success as a fledgling diplomat" (Foreman 1977). She later reported to congressional committees. The Senate sent a unanimously congratulatory telegram regarding her trip.

Americans supported Rosalynn Carter's trip, at least in retrospect. After her return, the president's pollster, Pat Caddell, reported to the president that "70 percent of Americans rated her journey as excellent or good" (Jensen 1990). At the conclusion of her trip, the *New York Times* editors decided that participation in foreign affairs was not beyond the range of activities in which the spouse of the president could appropriately be involved and they accepted the fact that Rosalynn Carter had done a creditable job.

> The initial reports suggest that Mrs. Carter did very well indeed at explaining her husband's interest, concern and policies and at eliciting extensive comments of both support and disagreement from her hosts. It is the quality of her ambassadorship that should concern us, not the range of subjects on

which the president might wish to exploit her prestige and proximity (*New York Times* 1977).

Solo international trips were rare for the two first ladies who preceded Hillary Rodham Clinton. In Ronald Reagan's two terms in the White House in the 1980s, Nancy Reagan took only three solo trips to three countries. During the Bush administration Barbara Bush traveled alone outside the United States only twice, to Costa Rica and to Canada.

HILLARY RODHAM CLINTON AND INTERNATIONAL POLITICS

As with so many other activities, Hillary Rodham Clinton has taken the role of foreign traveler in new and more policy-related directions both as a promoter of the Clinton administration foreign policy agenda and as an advocate for her own policy concerns regarding women and children. These trips have involved major speeches on women's rights, human rights, and democracy more generally. They often involved special meetings with women, especially meetings with women engaged in microenterprise businesses. She has also taken on a semi-official governmental role in announcing governmental aid packages to other countries.

Some observers have viewed her trips as an escape from domestic politics and couched them in the traditional goodwill mission role of the first lady. For example, Ann Devroy reporting on one of the first lady's early foreign visits described Hillary as "going about her public life as most first ladies do, . . . and this year for the first time, traveling abroad as a goodwill ambassador . . . Hillary Rodham Clinton, among the most untraditional of 20th century first ladies, gone publicly traditional this third year of her husband's presidency. Here in Chile in the midst of a five-day Latin American goodwill tour, Clinton could be Barbara Bush or Nancy Reagan or Rosalynn Carter in the framing of a message with all the sharp political edges rubbed smooth and with virtually universal appeal" (1995a, A1). But that perspective ignores the substantive messages she has delivered and the administration policy goals she has worked on during her many visits. For example, Troy Roberts on *CBS Morning News* described the same Latin America trip noted above as becoming "embroiled in controversy" when the first lady "issued her strongest criticism yet of threatened cuts in U.S. aid for foreign countries" (1995). Or note the following April 1999 description of her foreign policy ventures in the *Washington Post:*

> Forget the Senate. Over the last 12 days, Hillary Rodham Clinton has looked and sounded more like a candidate for Secretary of State. There she was in Egypt, gently urging tolerance for the minority Coptic Christians. There she was in Tunisia, lashing out at Islamic radicals in other countries who oppress women. And here she was in Morocco, speaking out on everything from the

Middle East peace process to the NATO airstrikes in Yugoslavia (Baker 1999, A17).

Her many trips have often been orchestrated to promote a foreign policy initiative of the executive office. The visits were coordinated with those of the secretary of state or UN ambassador as part of an administration plan. For example, administration officials described her 1996 trip to Central Europe as an engagement in a "good cop, bad cop" strategy with the UN ambassador. The first lady would generally speak in support of nongovernmental groups in nations with questionable support for democracy while the ambassador raised specific objections to governmental leaders regarding their human rights policies (Fournier 1996). Some of her trips have also been officially designated as diplomatic missions, in addition to her quasi-governmental role of presenting governmental aid programs to other nations as a representative of the administration.

Hillary Rodham Clinton had taken 21 solo foreign trips as first lady through the fall of 1999. (See list on p. 140.) She visited Latin and South America, Africa, Western and Eastern Europe, and Asia. She had visited U.S. troops, attended conferences on women's rights including her notable speech at the International Women's Rights Conference in Beijing in 1995, received awards, promoted United States interests, and stimulated goodwill more generally in her sightseeing tours of Africa and Asia.

The major themes of her trips have been women's rights, religious tolerance, and education, along with promotion and defense of U.S. foreign aid and the development of civil society through frequent praise and support of nongovernmental organizations (NGOs). The dominant message of her many speeches given in other nations has been that "human rights are women's rights and women's rights are human rights." She is tremendously popular overseas. (See, e.g., Hunt 1995; Devroy 1995a.) She has been introduced as "the first lady of the world" and been dubbed "queen of the world." Towns and schools have been named after her. The village of Rishi Para in Bangladesh, for example, changed its name to Hillary Para in 1995 after she met there with poor women who ran small businesses with loans from a rural bank. "Many people seem to see her as the voice of women's struggle for access to education, health care, jobs and credit, as well as freedom from violence" (Hunt 1995).

The policy perspectives of the first lady's trips can be put into five categories: 1) administration foreign policy goals, 2) promotion of foreign aid, 3) promotion of women's rights, 4) encouragement of the development and maintenance of civil societies, and 5) human rights advocacy in general. They are all clearly connected and not mutually exclusive efforts. The first lady's web page has included a section called At Work on Issues: Advancing Democracy, Civil Society, and Women's Full Participation Around the

World. That section divides the first lady's public pronouncements in this domain into seven areas: Human Rights (18), Civil Society (13), Women as Citizens (22), Health and Population Issues (11), Girls' Education (2), Microcredit (3), and US Engagement (21). The numbers in parentheses represent the listing of remarks, keynote addresses, and other such public speeches. that she has made around the world on these issues through mid-1999. (The numbers exclude her newspaper columns on these subjects.) Most have been made in other countries but some of the statements have been made at conferences, ceremonies, and other events held in the United States. This analysis of Hillary Rodham Clinton's international activities primarily uses news media commentary on her trips and her many speeches as "data." News media commentary has been obtained through the Lexis–Nexis on-line academic library. All of the first lady's speeches are available through her office's website.

FOREIGN POLICY GOALS AND THE FIRST LADY'S TRIPS

A review of news commentary regarding the purposes of her many trips provides a summary of the varied nature of her foreign policy missions for the president. For example, her 1995 trip to Mongolia was described as "part of American efforts to build close ties with [that nation] since it became independent from the former Soviet Union five years ago and adopted a democratic form of government." According to Assistant Secretary of State Winston Lord who accompanied the first lady on this trip, "Mrs. Clinton coming here demonstrates American support for Mongolian democracy and Mongolian independence" (Reuters 1995).

Mrs. Clinton traveled to Latin America in 1995 "to assess the progress of social reforms and build better ties between the United States and [those countries]" (Ross 1995). Her trip to Africa in 1997 was "designed to remind America that there is more to this vast continent than disease, war and famine" (Bulletin Broadfaxing Network). In Northern Ireland later that same year, she "urged all sides . . . to take risks for peace and promised Ireland's government . . . that the United States would remain deeply involved in the effort" (Associated Press).

In a 1997 review piece, *Newsweek* characterized the first lady as developing into a powerful presidential envoy "like her globetrotting hero Eleanor Roosevelt. . . . Like earlier trips to Africa, India and South America, Hillary's journey to Central Asia was no first lady photo op but a diplomatic mission crafted to promote American interests —as well as her own" (Breslau 1997).

Speaking to a conference on education prior to her visit, the first lady stated that the point of her 1997 trip to the former Soviet Union republics "is straightforward; to strengthen the young, but already strong, ties between our countries and to share ideas and experiences about ethnic and religious tolerance" (Kellman 1997a). It was reported that President Clinton had asked his wife to visit the region in his stead in order to promote economic and political stability in Central Asia, a region where democracy had yet to mature and an area where rich mineral resources remain untapped. She was also to promote American interests as some of the republics were considering striking trade oil deals with such nations as Iran and Iraq. (Kellman 1997a, 1997b). The *Washington Post* described that trip as a "mission of personal and cultural presence, she is at the cutting edge of a bold and little remarked aspect of Clinton foreign policy: to bring distant Central Asia and the Caucasus into what Deputy Secretary of State Strobe Talbott called the 'Euro-Atlantic community' when he laid out the policy in a speech last July. . . . Meanwhile we might pay a bit more attention to Mrs. Clinton, who is over there putting a distinctive face on American high policy" (Rosenfeld 1997). Thus, during the last five years of the Clinton administration the first lady traveled the world to promote specific and general aims of her husband's presidency and those aims were put forth quite publicly.

Promoting Foreign Aid.

Advocating United States engagement in world affairs through the judicious use of foreign aid has been a special focus of the messages the first lady has delivered abroad. She sought to counter Republican congressional attempts to reduce the level of foreign aid and engaged in an educational effort to create an interest on the part of the American public in the importance of foreign aid to the United States. On her 1995 Southeast Asia tour she stated, "I'm particularly pleased that much of our aid has gone to support this kind of enterprise. Too many people at home don't know the positive results that come from investments like this and don't know that something developed in Bangladesh can save lives in Louisiana" (Benac 1995). While touring a center for Mongolian street children benefiting from U.S. assistance, she pointed out that it showed the need for continued American foreign aid. "Many Americans do not know that we spend so little money helping other countries" (McQuillan 1995). And in Latin America, she chided those who would "walk away from investing in people." "I don't think it is a wise time for the United States to walk away from the accomplishments and achievements that have been made in working with governments and the private sector to improve the living conditions in Latin America" (Devroy 1995b). A year later she was urging Central and South American nations "to do more to combat maternal mortality," and she lamented that the Republican Congress had cut U.S. aid for such efforts (Sacramento Bee 1996).

The first lady not only promoted foreign aid on her international trips but also brought substantive aid packages with her. Among her duties during her foreign travels has been the announcement of U.S. foreign aid grants. This would appear to be the performance of a function that extends the position of first lady into that of a de facto government official serving as a U.S. representative. Her announcements of U.S. foreign aid initiatives have included:

- a $100 million U. S. initiative to increase female literacy and help girls in developing countries finish primary school.
- a $4.5 million aid package for Mongolia, a nation strategically located between China and Russia. The package included $3.5 million in aid to Mongolia's energy sector and one million dollars to UNICEF for a program to immunize Mongolian children and to fight pneumonia and diarrhea.
- a $5 million US Agency for International Development (USAID) grant to help the Pan American Health Organization combat maternal mortality, a daunting public health problem in Central and South America.
- a $8 million grant for primary education to fight illiteracy in Uganda.
- to help recover from hurricane Georges, an initial allocation of $5 million in emergency relief funds to Puerto Rico to begin repairs on roads and bridges, an additional $14.2 million to $35 million hurricane relief package to help Dominicans, and $2.1 million to a $12 million storm relief package to Haiti.
- a USAID grant of $50 million to enhance the construction of a civil society in southeastern Europe, of which $6 million was earmarked for non-governmental organizations in Bulgaria.
- a $50 million commitment through the U.S. Agency for International Development to support the common goals of this conference and the Summit of the Americas, to strengthen human rights, justice, and democracy, particularly on behalf of women.
- a $2 million USAID grant to work with the Pan American Health Organization to enable public health experts to determine how antibiotics are being misused and to train doctors and pharmacists in the correct way to administer prescription drugs.

Hillary Rodham Clinton and International Women's Rights.

In addition to advancing the foreign policy goals of her husband's administration through her numerous trips abroad, Hillary Rodham Clinton has had her own agenda of advocating for women's rights throughout the world. Her international messages expressed a strong feminism.

Early journalistic assessments of her presentations to domestic audiences critiqued their so-called feminist messages. In "A Feminism that Speaks for Itself" Tamar Lewin noted that Hillary had "been criticized for presenting too positive of a feminist image, emphasizing what women *can* do rather than what they are *kept from* doing, or their victimization" (1993). Some argue that Clinton's feminism is "a thing she has made acceptable to different political audiences" (Wills 1992), conveniently adopting the feminist mantle when it seems politically prudent to do so. According to Lewin, "What seems to be clear is that Clinton chooses to celebrate women's successes rather than their struggles. She still refuses to talk about women-as-victims, rarely talks about the women's movement, and ignores the largely feminist issues of abortion, equal pay, and domestic violence." She does, however, recognize powerful, successful women who have made a difference in politics and in society by mentioning and celebrating their achievements in many of her speeches (Muir and Benitiz 1996). Her international speeches, too, stressed the empowerment of women, but they also spoke to women's victimization. Her theme that "women's rights are human rights" could hardly avoid linking empowerment and victimization. In this domain she broadened the public face of her feminism.

Hillary Rodham Clinton began her international trips with a speech on March 8, 1995, at the International Women's Day observance in Copenhagen, Denmark, as part of a World Summit for Social Development. There she stressed the importance of education for women and girls and delivered the message that would be prominent throughout her international travels: United States engagement in world affairs and the improvement of women's lives in other countries are connected.

> "No single factor contributes to the long-term health and prosperity of a developing nation more than investing in education for girls and women. . . . Recognizing the critical role women must play in their own and their countries' development and the importance of education in enabling them to play that role, I am pleased to announce today that the United States will allocate $100 million over a 10-year period to provide enhanced educational opportunities for hundreds of thousands of girls and women in Africa, Asia, and Latin America who currently live in poverty. The goals of the initiative are ambitious: they include a 20% increase in girls' primary school completion rates or a 20% increase in the number of women who are functionally literate in the project areas in each country within 10 years."

On her Southeast Asia tour in that same month she declared "I believe we have to emphasize as much as possible that the denial of education, the denial of basic health care, the denial of basic choices to girls is a human rights issue" (Benac 1995).

Hillary's most dramatic, substantive, and prominent international venture during her tenure in the White House was the speech she gave at the International Women's Rights Conference in Beijing, China in September 1995. She forcefully condemned abuses of women and children in countries around the world and placed those violations of women's rights at the center of human rights concerns. "If there is one message that echoes forth from this conference," she said, "let it be that human rights are women's rights, and women's rights are human rights, once and for all." She deplored bride burnings in India, mass rapes in Bosnia, as well as the educational deprivation, coerced prostitution, genital mutilation, infanticide, and brutality that had been the lot of many of the world's women and girls. It is necessary, she said to "bring new dignity and respect to women and girls all over the world and thus bring new strength and stability to families as well."

Hillary Rodham Clinton's combining of the theme of empowerment of women and a condemnation of their victimization in her international speeches is well illustrated by her address to the United Nations on the occasion of International Women's Day in March 1999. Her theme of women's empowerment through broader educational and economic opportunities and better access to health care was prominent. "We are pleased to celebrate today that more women and girls are learning to read and write and, often for the first time, nations and families are investing in girls' education. We're also pleased that women are living longer and healthier lives and that more of us are surviving childbirth as we gain greater access to health care and reproductive services. We also see throughout the world that women are discovering a new level of economic independence. They're contributing more to their families and communities . . . more women are holding positions of power and authority." She gave instances of progress nations have made in these areas and noted examples of women leading peace efforts and making economic gains through access to microenterprise loans.

But her speech was also notable for its focus on the violation of women's rights around the world. "No nation can hope to move forward if its women and children are trapped in endless cycles of poverty, when they don't have the health care they need, when too many of them still die in childbirth, when they cannot read or take a job for which they will receive equal pay for equal work. . . . We can point to many problems around our world today where women—for reasons of history, culture, discrimination, prejudice—are used to lift up patriarchy, are used really as objects in order for others to exercise power . . . [it is] no longer acceptable to say that the abuse and mistreatment of women is cultural—it should be called what it is: criminal." She condemned the practices of the Taliban in Afghanistan and spoke in support of a United Nations protocol being negotiated on the trafficking of women and children.

In her trip to the former Soviet Union republics the first lady announced "a new White House–United Nations campaign against prostitution. "It is a violation of human rights when women are trafficked, bought and sold as prostitutes. We want to reach women who may be in danger" (*The Bulletin's Frontrunner*, November 19, 1997).

Her trips abroad were often centered on activities aimed to highlight a campaign for the empowerment of women. The Clinton administration has created a public/private partnership effort titled *Vital Voices* aimed at exploring ways of strengthening the role of women in new democracies and free-market economies. This effort has been promoted by Secretary of State Madeleine Albright with the active support of the first lady. *Vital Voices*, located within the USIA, is according to its website description "an ongoing global initiative, which implements U.S. Secretary of State Madeleine Albright's commitment to promote the advancement of women as a U.S. foreign policy objective." Its purpose is to create "unprecedented partnerships among governments, non–governmental organizations, and the private sector to support the full participation of women in the economic, social, and political progress of their countries."

Vital Voices has sponsored a number of international conferences to launch initiatives at which the first lady gave the keynote address. Further, the agenda of her foreign trips has usually included meetings with women, especially meetings with women engaged in businesses supported by microenterprise loans and grants. She has also taken part in annual meetings of the wives of heads of states in the Americas where her addresses have focused on the theme of empowerment of women.

Hillary Rodham Clinton has also stepped into the minefield of reproductive rights in her speeches in other nations. Most notable perhaps in this regard, was her address to the "Women of Argentina" in 1997. As described by Dan Rather on the CBS Evening News, "The first lady, Hillary Clinton, made headlines of her own in Argentina today—a passionate speech in that overwhelmingly Roman Catholic country—speaking out for birth control and the rights of women." The first lady stated that "Access to quality health care, especially family planning and reproductive heath services, is also crucial to advancing the progress of women." At the end of her remarks, pamphlets supportive of abortion rights rained down from theater boxes. The flyers said one thousand women have clandestine abortions every day in Argentina and at least one mother dies (Phillips 1997).

On nearly all of her trips, she has convened round-table discussions with local women's leaders about the challenges they face. She has made it a point to visit businesses created by women using microenterprise loans. She not only engaged in women's forums but has also participated in round-tables and intellectual exchanges with other heads of state. Illustrations of such exchanges include a 1997 trip to England in which the first lady participated in a closed seminar hosted by Prime Minister Tony Blair at Chequers. The seminar included participants from the United States and the United Kingdom focusing on shared policy perspectives and common challenges (U.S. Newswire official schedule for Hillary Rodham Clinton). She also spent time discussing world affairs with Czech political leaders on the invitation of Czech Republic President Vaclav Havel.

Civil Society.

Hillary Rodham Clinton's first address on civil society, according to her office's website, was given at the Radio Free Europe Headquarters in Prague, the Czech Republic, on July 4, 1996. There, addressing the fragile nature of the new democracies that had emerged from the Soviet Union empire, she talked about the development of "an alliance of democratic values to guide us as we confront the unavoidable questions of the 21st century." She said this was done by "building and strengthening civil society," a term she borrowed "from social scientists and philosophers who use it to describe the countless daily associations and actions that weave together the fabric of democratic life." As reported by Martha Teicher on the CBS Evening News, the first lady's aim in this visit to Eastern Europe was to "make the point that only by establishing independent bottom-up, non-governmental institutions can real democracy be built, and that American influence and aid dollars will be used to make that happen." In Slovakia at a round-table discussion with leaders of non-governmental organizations, she criticized the Slovak government for passing a law severely restricting grassroots political and cultural organizations. "I hope the government . . . will reconsider its opposition to the work of NGOs."

References to NGOs have become a standard feature of her international speeches. For example, visiting Macedonia in May 1999 at the end of the war to remove the Serbs from Kosovo, the first lady stated that when she arrived there she had "sat down with representatives from the NGOs such as CRS, UNHCR—many of the others who are on the frontlines." In June, she attended the Civitas Palermo World Conference: Making Education for Democracy an International Priority where she gave a keynote address in which she reiterated her position on the importance of the development and maintenance of democratic values that can only occur through citizens of different and diverse backgrounds working together in civic organizations. She often invoked the image that building and maintaining a democracy required not only a government of laws and a free market economy but also a civil society. That women played a key role in that civil society was frequently a central focus of her remarks.

Human Rights.

Her speeches regarding women's rights as noted above characterize the first lady's international remarks on human rights. She has also addressed human rights concerns beyond their specific effect on women globally. Her more general human rights perspective is illustrated by her remarks at the International Criminal Tribunal for Rwanda in March 1997,

> Genocide is a crime against humanity. The perpetrators of genocide must be brought to justice whenever genocide occurs; wherever genocide occurs. As a signatory of the International Convention on Genocide, the United States is legally and morally bound to prosecute and punish those who commit such crimes. But let me be clear: We seek punishment not for its own sake, but as a signal of the return of the rule of law and accountability, as a stark warning against future acts of horror, and as a first step on the road to peace and reconciliation.

CONCLUSION

Hillary Rodham Clinton has taken the traditional "goodwill ambassador" role of the first lady and made it a pointed, substantive, and integral part of the Clinton administration foreign policy efforts. The State Department has requested that she undertake some international trips to promote a foreign policy goal as part of a coordinated offensive in an area. Her strategy in these efforts has been to play an advocacy role in this arena usually addressing broad themes and sending messages rather than engaging in tense international politics in other nations.

When we think of Hillary Rodham Clinton's challenge to the traditional first ladyship, we have tended to focus on her domestic politics agenda and her effort to serve as formal policy advisor to her husband. But this examination of her role in international affairs and the foreign policy efforts of the Clinton administration shows an another dimension to her redefinition of the role of first lady. It many ways it is more in keeping with her predecessor Eleanor Roosevelt who was an advocate for rights on the world stage with whom Hillary has been connected than their domestic linkage.

On her foreign travels Hillary Clinton has combined the traditional goodwill ambassador role of first ladies, visiting historic sites, going on safaris, meeting with school children, and attending cultural events. with major speeches on controversial topics, promotion of her own political agenda, and advancing the foreign policy concerns of her husband's administration. She has sought to take women's rights from the sidelines of politics and place them squarely on center stage as an integral element of foreign policy agenda items. For the most part she has received little criticism for this involvement in executive branch politics and policy. She even received much praise from her usual conservative critics for her strong speech at the International Women's Rights Conference in Beijing in 1995. (See for example, Tang 1995).

It is difficult to know how much she has tried to influence the foreign policy direction of her husband's administration. For example, did she follow up her condemnation of human rights violations in China by trying to influence decisions about trade relations with that country? The Clinton administration did establish the president's Interagency Council on Women to coordinate the implementation of the Platform for Action adopted at the World Conference on Women in Beijing in 1995. Hillary Rodham Clinton serves as honorary chair of that council. But one can imagine that the clash between broad advocacy of human rights and specifically the condemnation of trafficking in women and the "real politik" of international trade and arms deals of a masculine administration would result in only incremental changes at best.

We can assume that, for the most part, she has engaged in the more traditional behind-the-scenes advocacy role of first ladies (although not so much in the foreign policy arena). Kenneth Walsh in a *U.S. News & World Report* article in 1997 noted on the issue of endorsing a worldwide treaty to ban land mines, that President Clinton let it be known that he heard the argument for endorsement "every night" from Hillary. "It turned out that Hillary Rodham Clinton had been waging her own lobbying effort against land mines [an effort that failed] in the privacy of the White House residence, without the knowledge of most of the president's other advisors" (26). Thus, we have both an expanded public role for the first lady in the international realm and evidence of traditional policy influence activities in that area in Hillary Rodham Clinton's actions. The way in which her participation in international events has been structured as formal diplomatic missions, deliverer of governmental aid and presidential envoy contribute to a transformation of the first lady and her office into a governmental position.

HILLARY CLINTON'S FOREIGN TRIPS AND STATED PURPOSE

1. Copenhagen, Denmark, March 1995—United Nation's Forum marking International Women's Day
2. Southern Asia, April 1995—12 day tour
3. China and Mongolia, Sept 1995—participation in United Nations Conference on Women
4. South America, October 1995—five-day visit—called by the White House an opportunity to act as a "strong spokesperson for the administration's commitment to fundamental social values"
5. Eastern Europe March 1996—ten-day trip to boost troop morale and spread her message of concern for women and children
6. Central Europe, July 1996—trip to stress the continued role of the United States in Central Europe

7. Bolivia, December, 1996—2 day trip—6th Conference of Wives of Heads of State and of Governments of the Americas

8. Africa, March 1997—two-week visit to give Africa a higher United States profile

9. Austria, July 1997—to participate in the Vital Voices Conference

10. Panama, October 1997—to attend Conference of Wives of Heads of States and of Governments of the Americas

11. Ireland, Northern Ireland and England, October 1997—to give speech on peace negotiations

12. Central Asia, November 1997—diplomatic mission to promote American interests

13. Geneva, May 1998—to receive United Arab Emirates Health Foundation prize at the World Health Assembly

14. Northern Ireland (a little ahead of Bill)—participate in the Vital Voices Conference

15. Chile and Uruguay, September 1998—"Vital Voices of the Americas: Women in Democracy" conference

16. Bulgaria, Czech Republic, October 1998—to attend International Women's Conference and Forum 2000, to promote women's rights and civil society

17. Central America, November 1998—hurricane

18. Netherlands, February 1999—to address the Hague Forum, an international population conference

19. Africa, March 1999—official diplomatic mission to promote U.S. interests and human rights

20. Northern Ireland, England, and Macedonia, May 1999—to receive honorary doctorate, National University of Ireland at Galway, to speak at London Conference on Human Rights for Children, to visit refugee camps in Macedonia

21. Iceland, October 1999—to speak at Vital Voices Conference

NOTE

1. This material on former first ladies first appeared in *The Other Elites*, edited by Janet Martin and Maryann Borrelli, Lynne Reiner, 1997.

Chapter 8

Conclusion: The First Lady and Equality for Women

What has the experience of Hillary Rodham Clinton's tenure as first lady and the people's response to her involvement in the Clinton presidency taught us about the mixing of the public and private in political leadership and the limits and possibilities of the position of first lady? What have we learned about the problem of the first ladyship? By the problem of the first ladyship, I mean the cultural imposition of a role on the spouse of a political leader that constrains that individual to the performance of limited functions and to serving as a role model for women playing a secondary role in society. She is not allowed to achieve on her own either within or outside the White House.

The problem is also about gender in politics. A gendered nature exists in the position of presidential spouse which conflicts with women being able to achieve as individuals and a presidential wife being able to take on a policy-making and advisory position in the presidential office. Men who have served as "first spouses" to women governors have not been expected to adopt host roles in the governors' mansions or to limit their own careers. We cannot ignore the fact that it has always been a woman in this position, which has created its gendered nature and impacted the mixing of the private and the public. Hillary Rodham Clinton desired a larger role as a presidential advisor and policy maker than had been traditional for first ladies. She did not wish to keep her influence behind the scenes as other first ladies have. Thus, she challenged the system.

This study of Hillary Rodham Clinton in the first ladyship has primarily utilized public opinion data to explore the limits and possibilities of the person in this role changing its nature from a supportive role emphasizing the private domain of the White House to being a part of the White House

143

policy advisory staff in a more formal capacity. In reaching some broad conclusions based on poll results, we need to consider responses to the polls in 1993 and in 1994 as the Clintons worked to implement their program of action and utilize the first lady as a public policy advisor and reflect upon reactions to Hillary Rodham Clinton's attempts to respond to that policy failure.

The results of the public opinion polls show or, perhaps more correctly, Hillary Rodham Clinton has shown as reflected by public opinion polls, that it is possible to be an activist first lady involved in public policy making, still be fairly popular, and not be seen as inappropriately influencing the president. This conclusion is based on public opinion polls in the *first* year of the Clinton administration. These polls also showed that the first lady will be viewed in partisan terms and will lose her ability to serve as a culturaly consensual figure. One has to determine if that loss is worth the effort to be part of a process of bringing about policy change. The polls also show hesitancy on the part of the U.S. public to abandon the traditional nonpolitical nature of the first ladyship and a preference for her not being a governmental official. But at the same time, if an individual first lady wishes to undertake a policy leadership position, the people respond positively to that effort, as they did when Hillary Rodham Clinton was initially named head of the president's health care task force. We need to keep in mind this mixed but primarily positive response to her activities, which occurred in 1993, as we assess the first ladyship for Hillary Rodham Clinton personally and for its position in the contemporary era.

The potential in Hillary Clinton's transformation of the first ladyship is reflected in Kathleen Hall Jamieson's conclusion that by her performance before Congress regarding the health care bill in September 1993, she had led:

> reporters and columnists [to inform] their readers that . . . [she] had widened the range of options open to future presidential spouses. . . . As the debate of the administration health care plan she helped to create comes to the fore, noted a New York Times caption, "Hillary Rodham Clinton is solidifying her position as power beside rather than behind, the throne." "The national consciousness has shifted, slightly but perceptible," noted Jan R. Esiner, the Philadelphia Inquirer's deputy editor for the editorial page. Hillary Clinton "proved the early critics wrong, and for that I believe, many women in this country are privately grateful." (1995, 47).

However, as I have chronicled, the "popular" first lady became quite unpopular in the second year of the administration. The Clintons faltered both in the substance of the health care plan that they put before Congress and in the process that they used to develop that plan. The political opposition undermined their popularity in 1994 by keeping the issue of their involvement in the Whitewater development project before the public. In the end they had to withdraw their health care proposal from congressional consideration. Since the president's wife had taken the lead in this effort, she had to share responsibility for its demise. Her popularity declined and support for an activist first lady generally diminished. Hillary Rodham Clinton struggled since that time to redirect her activist efforts as first lady to regain her popularity, not really succeeding until she performed a very traditional role of the supportive and forgiving wife during the Lewinsky affair of 1998.

Would it have been better had President Clinton never appointed his wife to lead the task force? In assessing this question, we must consider the implications had the outcome of the task force been different; what if the Clintons had been successful in enacting into law some type of health care reform? Clearly the first ladyship would have been transformed. The important point here is that public opinion polls showed substantial support for a person undertaking that transformation, although it also implies that she could probably only achieve a redefinition if at the same time she did not neglect or show contempt for the traditional ceremonial, hostess, and homemaker duties of the first lady. Hillary Rodham Clinton worked hard to combine both roles, which often confused journalists covering her but probably helped to sustain a positive relationship with the public in the first year.

In some ways President Clinton's appointment of Hillary Rodham Clinton as head of the health care task force was exactly the right thing to do to move beyond the constrainiment of political wives to secondary roles. This appointment in her husband's administration allowed her to seek to accomplish something through her own abilities (which is not to ignore the political reality that other actors in the process would still respond to her in a special and deferential way because she was the wife of the president). Of course, she was given the position because she was the president's spouse, but advisors are often given positions because they are long-time confidants of the president. Personal relationships are always part of the selection of advisors as well as more objective credentials. In Hillary's case, it was not as if the job was given to someone who had never been involved in the policy-making process. She had far more than her wedding ring as a credential, although health care was not her forte. We should recall the earlier discussion in this book that she was viewed as being qualified for a high level position in a Democratic administration if her husband had not been president.

Unfortunately, for breaking the cultural constraints of the first ladyship, Hillary Rodham Clinton failed in her effort to achieve a policy triumph for her husband and allowed herself to become a target for the political right, contributing to the undermining of her husband's ability to lead the nation.

After the disastrous 1994 midterm elections for Democrats, Hillary was made to rethink her role and would not take on a formal policy-making position in the rest of administration. The Clintons did briefly flirt with the idea of her taking a leading role in welfare reform efforts during and after the 1996 election but that received an overwhelmingly negative response in the media. She was given lots of advice in the media as to what she should do and what the first ladyship should be about. Advice focused both on her role in this position and reflections on the first ladyship more generally during this time period.

Supporters of an activist first lady for the most part suggested that Hillary Rodham Clinton should continue to be a national advocate for the causes she believed in but should not attempt to be a policy maker. For example, journalist Gloria Borger speaking on *Inside Politics* suggested, "I wouldn't advise the White House to put Hillary Rodham Clinton in charge of a welfare reform task force right now, as she did for health care. But on, the other hand, I think people are also saying, being in an advisory capacity, being in an outspoken capacity—there's nothing wrong with that" (November 30, 1994). Anna Quindlen (1994c) and Doris Kearns Goodwin (1994) advocated her becoming a spokesperson for outsiders in the style of Eleanor Roosevelt. Her public activities in 1995 indicated that is exactly the route she decided to take although especially her internationalism took the first ladyship into a new sphere of policy involvement.

Others believe the first lady should sacrifice any public opinions that she might have and any ideas of a political partnership to concentrate on being a nonpolitical symbol which Americans seem to need. Betsy Hart, writing in the *Rocky Mountain News*, illustrates this position, "For while the president must play politics and to a certain extent be divisive, we rely on a first spouse—until now first ladies—to unite us; to be someone we all can look to respect and claim as our own. We want the first spouse to be someone all Americans can cheer, like Barbara Bush or Jackie Kennedy. Not someone who herself (or himself) is embroiled in divisive political fights" (1994). Advocates of this position, however, fail to tell us why it is that the spouse of a chief executive must take on this role. A variant of this theme has been expressed by former First Lady Barbara Bush who said the first lady should keep her opinions to herself as she was not elected, her husband was. The constraints on the first lady go against our culture of individual achievement. Barbara Bush does have a point, however, if the media are only interested in the first lady's opinions because she happens to be the spouse of the president rather than having been involved in the political process in her own right.

Others argue that the entire idea of a "first lady" is outdated and even contrary to a democratic society. Few other western democratic countries expect the wives of their political leaders to serve as national hostesses and advocates. Germaine Greer, writing in *The New Republic* (1995), advocated abolishing the first ladyship. The notion of a "first lady" according to Greer has more to do with royalty and hereditary systems of rulership than with democracies which elect individuals to public office. She believes presidents' spouses should be freed to lead private lives and pursue careers of their own: "No woman anywhere will be expected to relinquish her privacy and her own work, to diet and dress up and give interviews every day, simply because she has married a man who has a prospect of success in politics." This individualistic perspective very much represents the philosophy of the contemporary feminist movement. A.M. Rosenthal in the *New York Times* has made a similar point: ". . . it is a job that should not exist. It is philosophically twisted in concept and it is politically outrageous in practice. In concept, the first ladyship is an affront to American democracy— and to American feminism" (1994).

But we have moved in the opposite direction regarding presidents' spouses. The contemporary first lady has an office allocated to her and a budget appropriated for her assistance to the president by the U.S. Congress (although no salary) as a consequence of the White House Personnel Authorization–Employment Act of 1978 as discussed in Chapter 5. Thus, her position has expanded and become more formal. Even the fact that she has been given a "title," official in the sense that government manuals now list the Office of First Lady as part of the president's office and is not just known as the wife of the president suggests a governmental position. She is assumed to have official duties. The judiciary has proclaimed her a "de facto" government official. Pollsters even ask the public to evaluate the "job" she is doing. But our culture constrains those duties and that job and confines the person in this position to seemingly nonpolitical public roles such as being first hostess and representing the president at ceremonial functions. What happens when that individual, rather than being a private person with a career of her own or performing the homemaker role out of the public eye or being the first hostess, is a political advisor and has a desire to be involved in policy making? Automatically denying her that opportunity conflicts with the premises of our individual achievement oriented society.

If we did away with the formal position of first lady following Germaine Greer's call and treated the president's spouse as an individual, then perhaps she (or he) would be free to assume a political advisory position in the administration or even serve in the cabinet if she had the professional background or political credentials to assume such a position as well as pursue a career outside the White House. She could be evaluated on her own merits in the tradition of our individual achievement culture. Movement in this direction of abolishing the position of first lady would eliminate at least to a degree the problem of mixing private and public spheres. Less of the spouse's role in governing would flow from her private relationship with the chief executive and more would come from, shall we say, public or political achievement, emanating from her own professional credentials. The fact that she is the spouse becomes secondary, although of course the special intimacy of the husband and wife relationship can not be removed entirely. And the advantage she would have vis-a-vis other advisors would probably continue to cause consternation within the office of the president. But by its nature the office of the president is filled with jealousies and competition for influence with or without the involvement of the president's spouse.

Of course, it is unrealistic to expect that the "first ladyship" could be banished. It was not created by an act of Congress. It is a cultural tradition that has developed over time and gradually has become institutionalized as part of government. Congress might rescind that section of Public Law 95–570, the White House Personnel Authorization–Employment Act of 1978 that authorizes funds for a presidential spouse to assist her husband and provides a certain amount of legitimization for her office in the White House. The social apparatus of the White House rather than being institutionalized under the first lady's domain should be reconstructed to report to the president's chief-of-staff through some line of authority. The president could organize the White House office so that it does not include an Office of the First Lady.

It is hard to imagine, however, these actions being taken. Even with all of its cultural constraints the first ladyship provides the individual with a great deal of influence if she wishes to exercise it. Therefore, little incentive is present for an individual today to renounce assumption of that role. Thus, we must assess the expansion of this position and evaluate possibilities for its alteration into part of the president's advisory staff.

Some have suggested that President Clinton raised a constitutional issue in appointing Hillary head of the task force in that he skirted the Bobby Kennedy law. (See, for example, Hoff 1996; Rosenthal 1994.) Since she received no pay, technically he did not violate it. Also the law states that "a public official may not appoint, employ, promote, [or] advance a relative in an agency in which he is serving or over which he exercises jurisdiction or control. . . ." But does the appointment to a staff position as an advisor within the White House not to an executive branch agency constitute "appointment to an agency" as described in Chapter 5?

President Clinton might have shown more respect for the legislative process by speaking to the problems that law creates for presidents, noting perhaps among other things, its limit on the president's freedom to obtain assistance from people close to him, its insult to his ability to choose competent advisors, and the ability of the U.S. public to render judgment on the president's competency in his choice of his assistants based on their actions.

What President Clinton might have done was to raise the issue and have legislation introduced into Congress to rescind the "Bobby Kennedy" law suggesting that it take effect after his administration. Such an action might have shown respect on his part for the lawmaking process.

The "Bobby Kennedy" law was originally passed in spite by the Johnson administration after President Kennedy had appointed his brother to be attorney general, a man whom Lyndon Johnson intensely disliked and viewed as a political rival. It could be pointed out that the president is free to appoint any cronies he wishes to staff positions in the White House but not his brother, uncle, or mother. He could even, one supposes, appoint his mistress but not his wife. What if Bill and Hillary were to divorce as the tabloids have occasionally suggested? Could he then appoint her to be attorney general or secretary of education (maybe even as part of the divorce settlement)? Of course that seems ridiculous, but it is an extension of the logic of the prohibition of this piece of legislation on presidential appointments. One could even take it one step further and imagine that had Bill and Hillary never gotten married but only lived as partners, he would have had no legal limitations on appointing her to an executive branch position. It is a separate question as to whether the public would have been ready to accept such a living arrangement in a presidential candidate. But such arrangements have become more and more an accepted part of contemporary life.

In evaluating the idea of the first lady as playing a role as a public presidential advisor, the issue of accountability has been raised. Some observers have suggested a lack of accountability exists when the first lady becomes involved in public policy. For example, journalist Maureen Dowd made this point in an October 1995 *New York Times* editorial critical of Hillary Clinton for taking on a policy-making role: "When she came to Washington, Mrs. Clinton appeared to willfully ignore the political dangers of assigning herself so much power with no accountability. . . . She thinks Americans fear the partnership with her husband. What they really fear is a bargain that ignores accountability. It's not about being a woman. It's about not being elected." Or note Meg Greenfield's comment regarding Rosalynn Carter's public policy advisory role, "Mrs. Carter, by her very seriousness of purpose, is inviting an end to this facade of deference. She is asking to be part of the political and governing process, and the answer to whether or not she *should* do that is this: only if she agrees to make herself accountable in the ordinary way" (1977).

But does little accountability exist for a presidential spouse who "works" in her husband's administration? Does her level of accountability differ from that of other advisors? What are the ways in which the first lady can be held accountable? In advocating for a role for her in the public policy-making process, we must assess the presence and effectiveness of any means by which she can be held accountable. A major element of account-ability would be receiving a salary and being subject to being fired for not performing the job according to the wishes of the president. The nation has chosen not to provide a salary for the spouse of the president for the per-formance of her overall duties as hostess plus advisor, nor can she be paid because of the "Bobby Kennedy" law for any particular task that she undertakes for the president. No formal means of firing her exist either. But she can be dismissed from a position as Hillary essentially was from the Health Care Task Force, and the mini-furor that arose from the idea of her taking on welfare reform in 1996 kept her from assuming that position.

Some informal ways do exist by which she can be held accountable, probably even more so than most presidential advisors. First is the fact that she is the person "closest to the president." Thus, her activities reflect most directly on him and his presidency. Her performance will affect evaluation of him more immediately than that of any other advisor. Her incompetence, particularly given the gendered context in which it will be viewed, will harm him to a greater degree than other administration blunders. Second is the fact that the first lady's actions receive immense press scrutiny. There is little that she could do as a public advisor that will not be publicized and analyzed in news stories, editorials, and nightly news commentary. This indirect form of accountability plays a major role in keeping the first lady accountable for her actions. If she only advises behind the scenes within the facade of playing the hostess role, she has much less accountability. It would be also unnatural to expect that no presidential spouse would offer advice and be involved in the workings of the administration. First ladies have a long history of being engaged as political partners to their husbands.

What if we were to think of the appointment of a presidential spouse to an advisory position as making that individual a quasi-member of the White House office staff? I use the term "quasi" only because of the inabil-ity to pay a spouse a salary. If her advisory post were to be considered a staff position, she would be held to the same accountability standards as other staff members. (This, of course, ignores the greater reticence some might have to raise questions about the performance of the presidential wife as opposed to that of other staff members, but such hesitation reflects back to our discussion of the first lady as an icon that has caused problems for equality in contemporary times.)

What then are the general mechanisms for holding White House staff accountable? Holding presidential staff accountable has been a source of consternation within Congress and among students of the presidency. It has not been an easily resolvable issue. (See, e.g., Hart 1987.) The potential for holding presidential staff accountable comes primarily through congres-sional oversight mechanisms. The most immediate means relevant for our purposes here is Congress's right to hold hearings and investigations into executive branch activities. According to presidential scholar John Hart, hearings and investigations have been the most visible forms of congressional oversight and one of the primary means by which it has held the officials who manage the departments and agencies of the executive branch accountable.

> Those whose appointments in government are established by law are expected to testify before congressional committees when asked to do so, and their testimony, and the information it provides, is considered vital to the effective performance of the oversight function. Presidential staff have been treated as an exception in this respect because of their close relationship with the president, and the doctrine of executive privilege is invoked to exclude them from the requirement to testify before Congress. The rationale for this is simply that presidents need the best advice available, and that advice might not be given so freely if advisors were denied the protection of confidentiality and ultimately forced to account in a public forum for the advice given.
>
> That rationale is less applicable, and claims of executive privilege more questionable, when presidential aides become policymakers in their own right, as has happened in recent decades (145). . . . Existing law makes it a misdemeanor, punishable by a fine and imprisonment, for anyone to refuse to appear as a witness if summoned by Congress and to refuse to answer any pertinent question. There is no specific exemption in the law for the presidential staff, not even for the president's personal staff in the White House Office. In terms of the strict letter of the law, it would seem that the presidential staff have no right to refuse to attend a congressional committee hearing and, if they refused to answer any pertinent question on the basis of executive privilege, than, because a misdemeanor would have been committed, the matter would have to be resolved in the courts, and it would be up to the courts to determine the claim of executive privilege. But Congress has been reluctant to push the issue into the courts, and the effect of that reluctance has left the White House staff the sole arbiters of when the doctrine of executive privilege should be invoked (146).

In her capacity as head of the Health Care Task Force, Hillary Rodham Clinton should have been held accountable by Congress's ability to call her to come before them to describe and defend her actions in that position, but, as Hart has told us, Congress has been reluctant in general to pursue this avenue to hold White House staff accountable. But it does not follow that the first lady is uniquely not held accountable for her actions in this position.

In the end, to argue against the president's spouse being able to take on a policy-making role in the executive branch is to constrain women from playing an equal role in the political life of the nation. The challenge is to alter that position and the way that we think about people in it so that spouses can achieve in their own right whether that achievement is in pur-

suit of a profession divorced from the presidency or whether it is performing a key function in the administration. How much better for women if
the spouse is not seen as manipulating policy behind the scenes and does
not have to pretend to put a bag over her head and have no opinions as
Hillary Rodham Clinton has noted. She should be allowed to choose what
to do with her life.

The theme of choice became a notable refrain in the public statements
of the candidates' wives in 1992 in the aftermath of Marilyn Quayle's
"essential natures" comment in her speech at the 1992 Republican convention. To calm the controversy swirling around her earlier comment,
Quayle wrote in a follow-up piece "We don't have to reject the prospect of
marriage and children to succeed. We don't have to reject our essential
natures as women to prosper in what was once the domain of men. It is no
longer an either-or situation." According to Barbara Bush, "everyone's different and that's a great thing." Hillary Clinton repeated as often as possible the statement that each woman should choose what is best for her.
When asked by Larry King whether she had changed the pattern for first
ladies, Clinton responded,

> Larry, I don't think there should be a pattern. I really think that each indi-
> vidual ought to be free to do what she thinks is best for herself and her hus-
> band and her country. I have a lot of respect for all the women who have been
> in this position and I think every one of them made a significant contribution,
> but they may have done it in a different way. . . . Everybody should be per-
> mitted to be who they are" (Jamieson 1995, 44–45).

In an interview with reporters at the conclusion of her five-day Latin
American tour in October 1995, Clinton reiterated this theme. "First
ladies, she said, are caught in an 'inevitable double bind,' attacked if they
are too active and if they are not active enough. Her plea for her succes-
sors, she said, is that they be allowed to work out any kind of convention-
al or unconventional role in a world where women's roles are changing. A
first lady, she said, should be allowed to be an activist or 'not do anything
at all'" (Devroy 1995b).

Thus, if it is accepted that every woman should choose what is best for
her, then why shouldn't the first lady be able to choose to be a political
partner and policy-making advisor to the president? Why should Hillary
Rodham Clinton have to relinquish the role, she had performed in
Arkansas once she moved to Washington?

To what degree does it matter more broadly what role the spouse of the
president plays and what positions she assumes in an administration? The
first lady's role has been as an icon for an ideal of American womanhood.
It is steeped in public and private traditions that have driven political phi-

losophy and constrained women from being able to attain individual achievement. If the first lady were freed from those cultural limitations, it would represent an egalitarian step forward for American women. The symbolic importance of freeing political wives would be large. It might help political husbands, as well.

The vast majority of Americans have expressed support for the idea of women in political leadership positions. In 1987, 82 percent expressed approval when asked in a Gallup poll, "If your party nominated a woman for president, would you vote for her if she were qualified for the job?" And in another Gallup poll in 1984, 91 percent said they would vote for a woman for Congress. The debate that Hillary Rodham Clinton engendered during the 1992 presidential campaign distracted from the record number of women running for public office that year. Some commentators derisively called it the "Year of the Wife," rather than the "Year of the Woman," which had the intended impact of hurting the cause of liberal equality for women. The debate about the political influence of the first lady detracts from the ability of women seeking elective and appointive office. It continues to confuse the private and public and stresses gendered roles. The first ladyship is an old-fashioned idea that conflicts with contemporary beliefs in women's equality and women's quests for political leadership. Hillary Rodham Clinton's tenure in the White House has made that very clear. "Whatever Mrs. Clinton's other troubles, her biggest problem is institutional. She is a '90s woman trying to function in a '50s role" (Lehigh 1996).

The problem is how to treat the spouse of the president as an individual, to free her from the cultural constraints that have been imposed on this role. Constraints that have been placed on the presidential spouse's acting in the public sphere contradict the liberal tradition of individualism that has characterized American social and political culture. The individual is at the center of liberal democracy, but patriarchy has limited woman's opportunities. Drawing on Susan Okin, Campbell has noted that ". . . despite contemporary commitments to individualism, there is a long tradition that brings the family and woman's traditional role in it into conflict with individual rights" (1993, 10). Behind the individual rhetoric of liberal philosophers "it is clear that the family and not the adult human individual is the basic political unit" (Okin, 1979, 282). Because of her position in the family, the first lady is not able to act as an autonomous, independent individual. She may be credited with political influence but it is an influence hidden behind a mask of domesticity and is treated with considerable suspicion.

Liberal feminism is based upon the premise "that women are individuals possessed of reason, that as such they are entitled to full human rights, and that they should therefore be free to choose their role in life and explore their full potential in equal competition with men" (Bryson 1992, 159). Freeing the first lady of cultural constraints so she can pursue her own career means not only an ability to work outside the White House but the opportunity to serve as a presidential advisor if that is the job she desires and can lay professional claim to.

Hillary Clinton's tenure as first lady has placed the presidential spouse as a key player in the presidential White House. Therefore, as the Clinton presidency concludes, we can begin to think about the impact of her years as first lady and her legacy on that position. We can ask the extent to which Hillary Rodham Clinton has freed presidential spouses from the gender constraints that have been placed on that position. Is a person in this position more likely to serve as an autonomous individual in keeping with liberal democratic premises because of Hillary's efforts?

Hillary Rodham Clinton has provided future spouses with both greater leeway for how they will approach this "job" and set up hurdles for them. She has loosened some of the gender constraints but made them more visible. They cannot be ignored, and the extent to which women have been the base of her support suggests that for the most part women want those constraints removed. This suggests certain changes in their own lives and ambitions.

Hillary has not been totally in control of her destiny as first lady. We have seen that events outside of her control have had a major impact on her relationship with the public, namely the Whitewater investigation and the sexual escapades of her husband. The former made her seem a liability on the administration and the latter made her an asset. The first lady can certainly be criticized for not handling the Whitewater investigation better and for not doing a better job of selling the Clinton health care plan, efforts that would have enhanced her relationship with the American public. Future presidential spouses can learn from that experience how to use the opportunities available to them to communicate their goals. One could look to Lady Bird Johnson and her press secretary Liz Carpenter's efforts for examples of how to communicate through the media (Foreman 1971).

The first impression that one might take away from an overview of Hillary's years is not to attempt to be an overt policy advisor to the president. This would be a misreading of her history, as the polls have indicated. One would have to more sensitively craft her position. Certainly future spouses will hesitate to take on a formal position. We can also imagine that given the increasing numbers of women with professional backgrounds that women will increasingly chafe at the gender limitations of the position of first lady and continue to call its premises into question. More presidential spouses will want to continue to pursue their independent careers, which will continue to be difficult given potential conflicts of interest.

In reflecting upon the puzzle of presidential spousal politics we have to take into account the sexual and gender biases that influence our thinking and consider the presidential advisory system as a whole. We have to place that individual in the context of a quest for equal rights and political involvement for women. In the end to argue against the president's spouse having the opportunity to take on a policy-making role or to achieve as an individual and setting constraints because of her sex and her gender contributes to keeping women from playing an equal role in the political domain.

References

Alvarez, Lizette. "Hillary Clinton: Popular, and Hardly in Hiding." *New York Times*, August 12, 1998: A1.

Anthony, Carl Sferrazza. *First Ladies: The Saga of the Presidents' Wives and Their Power, 1789–1961*. New York: William Morrow and Company, 1990.

Anthony, Carl Sferrazza. *First Ladies: The Saga of the Presidents' Wives and Their Power, 1961–1990*. New York: William Morrow and Company, 1991.

Arkansas Democrat Gazette. "Overseas, Women See Hillary Clinton as Their Champion." September 10, 1995: 7A.

Associated Press. "Hillary Rodham Clinton Urges Risks for Peace in Northern Ireland." October 30, 1997.

Baker, Paula. *The Moral Frameworks of Public Life: Gender, Politics, and the State in Rural New York, 1870–1930*. New York: Oxford University Press, 1991.

Baker, Peter. "In Morocco, Hillary Clinton Discards Politics for Diplomacy." *The Washington Post*, April 1, 1999: A17.

Barrett, Mark. "Elizabeth Dole Stressing Contrast to Mrs. Clinton at Appearances." *Asheville Citizen-Times*, May 20, 1996: Local A1.

Baldrige, Letitia. *Of Diamonds and Diplomats*. Boston: Houghton Mifflin Company, 1968.

Bardes, Barbara, and Suzanne Gossett. *Declarations of Independence: Women and Political Power in Nineteenth Century American Fiction*. New Brunswick, N. J.: Rutgers University Press, 1990.

Beasley, Maurine. *Eleanor Roosevelt and the Media*. Chicago: University of Illinois Press, 1987.

Beck, Joan. "Hillary: Powerhouse or White Housewife?" *Chicago Tribune*, November 19, 1992: 21.

Benac, Nancy. "First Lady Winds Up 12-Day Visit to Indian Subcontinent. Associated Press, April 4, 1995.

Benedetto, Richard. "Wynette Remark Shows Democrats Once Again Misread Millions." *Gannett News Service*. January 31, 1992.

Benedetto, Richard. "Activist Role Wins Approval." *USA Today*, October 1, 1993: 1.

Benedetto, Richard. "First Lady Receives Her Best Poll Results in Year." *USA TODAY*, August 30, 1996: 6A.

Black, Allida. WWW H-Net Discussion List for American Political History Affairs of States, Monday, Sept. 22, 1997.

Boylan, James. "The Scarlet W." *Columbia Journalism Review*. January/February, 1995: 53–60.

Brant, Martha. "Cashing In on Letting Hillary Be Hillary." *Newsweek*. September 2, 1996: 24.

Breslau, Karen. "Destination Unknown" *Newsweek*, November 14, 1997: 45–46.

Broder, David. "New Kind of Ground Rules for a First Lady." *Washington Post*, November 29, 1992: C7.

Broder, David. "Looking for Leadership, Voter Rage Cools, Worries Remain." *Washington Post*, November 6, 1995: Sec A1.

Brodie, Ian. "First Lady Takes Charge." *The Ottawa Citizen*, October 27, 1998: A10.

Buhle, Mari Jo, and Paul Buhle. *The Concise History of Woman Suffrage*. Urbana: University of Illinois Press, 1978.

Bulletin Broadfaxing Network. "First Lady's Africa Trip a Success." March 24, 1997.

Bulletin's Frontrunner, November 19, 1997.

Bumiller, Elizabeth. "THE OTHER DOLE—a Special Report; Elizabeth Dole Is Eager to Keep Strength Subtle." *New York Times*, July 16, 1996a: A1.

Bumiller, Elizabeth. "Running Against Hillary." *New York Times Magazine*, October 13, 1996b: 37+.

Burrell, Barbara. *A Woman's Place Is in the House: Campaigning for Congress in the Feminist Era*. Ann Arbor: The University of Michigan Press, 1994.

Campbell, Karlyn Kohrs. *Man Cannot Speak for Her*. Westport, Conn.: Greenwood Press, 1989.

Campbell, Karlyn Kohrs. "Shadowboxing with Stereotypes: The Press, the Public, and the Candidates' Wives." Research Paper R–9. Cambridge, Mass.: John F. Kennedy School of Government, 1993.

Campbell, Karlyn Kohrs. "The Discursive Performance of Femininity: Hating Hillary." *Rhetoric and Public Affairs.* 1, Spring, 1998: 1–20.

Campbell, Steve. "Hillary Clinton Encourages High Schoolers; In Addition to Discussing Education Issues, The First Lady Urges More Women to Vote." *Portland Press Herald,* October 1, 1996: 1B.

Cannon, Angie. "Hillary Clinton Suffers a Year of Heavy Criticism." *Philadelphia Inquirer,* September 16, 1994: 7.

The Capital Times. "A First Lady's Global View." April 8, 1995: Sec. A.

Carlson, Margaret. "The Dynamic Duo." *Time,* January 4, 1993a: 39–41.

Carlson, Margaret. "At the Center of Power," *Time,* May 10 1993b: 29–36.

Caroli, Betty Boyd. *First Ladies.* New York: Oxford University Press, 1995.

Carroll, Ginny. "Will Hillary Hurt or Help?" *Newsweek,* March 30,1992:30–31.

Carter, Rosalynn. *First Lady from Plains.* Boston: Houghton Mifflin, 1984.

Castaneda, Carol, and Brian O'Donnell. "Women, Youth Rate Hillary Clinton Highest." *USA TODAY.* March 24, 1992.

Clift, Eleanor. "Hillary Then and Now." *Newsweek,* July 20, 1992a: 38–39.

Clift, Eleanor, and Mark Miller. "Hillary: Behind the Scenes." *Newsweek,* December 28, 1992: 23–25.

Clines, Francis. "From Political Debit to Force: Hillary Clinton," *New York Times,* November 11, 1998: A1.

Clymer, Adam. "Hillary Clinton Says Administration Was Misunderstood on Health Care." *New York Times,* October 3, 1994.

Cohen, Richard. "The Hillary Clinton Factor." *The Washington Post,* March 18, 1992: A21.

Converse, Jean, and Stanley Presser. *Survey Questions: Handcrafting the Standardized Questionnaire.* Newbury Park, Calif.: Sage Publications, 1986.

Cooper, Matthew. "The Hillary Factor." *U.S. News & World Report,* April 27, 1992: 32–37.

Cooper, Matthew. "Co-President Clinton?" *U.S. News & World Report.* February 8, 1993: 30–32.

Corcoran, Katherine. "Pilloried Clinton." *Washington Journalism Review.* January/February, 1993: 27–29.

CQ Almanac. Washington, D.C.: Congressional Quarterly Press, 1978.

Creager, Ellen. "Some Say She's the One Who Should Be President." *Detroit Free Press,* January 14, 1992.

Davis, Anna Byrd. "Hillary Clinton's Support Booms." *Tennessee Commercial Appeal,* March 22, 1993.

Devroy, Ann. "First Lady's Softer Focus Follows Drop in Popularity; on LatinTour, Traditional Role is Revived." *Washington Post,* October 15, 1995a: A1.

Devroy, Ann. "First Lady Advocates 'Investing in People'; GOP Social Cuts Apparent Aim of Remarks." *Washington Post,* October 16, 1995b: A16.

Devroy, Ann. "First Lady Denounces Her Critics." *Milwaukee Journal Sentinel,* October 18, 1995c: 1.

Diamond, Edwin, Gregg Geller, and Heidi Ruiz. "Watching the Hillary-Watchers . . . Shows How Coverage Has Changed." *National Journal,* April 24, 1993: 1004–5.

Dinkin, Robert. *Campaigning in America.* New York: Greenwood Press, 1995.

Dobbin, Muriel. "Now It's Hillary Clinton to the Rescue." *Sacramento Bee,* October 27, 1998: A1.

Dowd, Maureen. "The 1992 Campaign Trail: From Nixon, Predictions on the Presidential Race." *New York Times,* February 6, 1992: Sec. A.

Dowd, Maureen. "Return to Gender." *The New York Times.* October 19, 1995: A25.

Drew, Elizabeth. *On the Edge: the Clinton Presidency.* New York: Simon and Schuster, 1994.

Drew, Elizabeth. *Whatever it Takes.* New York: Viking Press, 1997.

Duerst-Lahti, Georgia. "Reconceiving Theories of Power: Consequences of Masculinism in the Executive Branch." In *The Other Elites: Women, Politics, and Power in the Executive Branch.* Ed. Janet Martin and Maryanne Borrelli. New York: Lynne Reiner, 11–32, 1997.

Duerst-Lahti, Georgia and Rita Mae Kelly. *Gender Power, Leadership and Governance.* Ann Arbor: University of Michigan Press, 1995.

The Economist "Hillary Clinton, Trail-Blazer." December 5, 1992: 30.

Edwards, George, and Stephen Wayne. *Presidential Leadership.* New York: St Martin's Press, 1985.

Egan, Timothy. "New Idaho Community Raises Neighbors' Fears." *The New York Times,* October 5, 1994: A18.

Elshtain, Jean Bethke. "Moral Woman and Immoral Man: A Consideration of the Public-Private Split and Its Political Ramifications." *Politics and Society.* 4, 1974:453–473.

Elshtain, Jean Bethke. "Aristotle, the Public-Private Split, and the Case of the Suffragists." In *The Family in Political Thought,* ed. Jean Bethke Elshtain. Amherst: University of Massachusetts Press, 1982.

Evans, Sara. *Born for Liberty.* New York: The Free Press, 1989.

Fineman, Howard, and Mark Miller. "Hillary's Role." *Newsweek,* February 15, 1993: 18–23.

Fogarty, Thomas. "Iowans Give Thumbs Up to First Lady." *Des Moines Register*, May 3, 1993.

Foreman, Laura. "Mrs. Carter Leaves on Latin Tour Today." *New York Times*. May 30, 1977: A.

Foreman, Laura. "Mrs. Carter Home, Gets Husband's Seal of Approval." *New York Times*, June 13, 1977: A.

Foreman, Norma Ruth Holly. "The First Lady as a Leader of Public Opinion: A Study of the Role and Press Relations of Lady Bird Johnson." Ph.D. Dissertation. University of Texas, Austin, 1971.

Fournier, Ron. "First Lady Nudges Slovak Government to Ease Policy on Private Groups." Associated Press, 1996a.

Fournier, Ron. "Clintons Work on Speeches, Other Ideas for Convention; First Lady Will Have Prominent Role." *Austin American-Statesman*, August 17, 1996b.: A13

Frisby, Michael. "Large Role for Mrs. Clinton No Longer Troubles Most Americans." *Wall Street Journal,* December 18, 1992: A6.

Gallup, George. "Mrs. Roosevelt More Popular Than President, Survey Finds." *Washington Post*, January 15, 1939.

Garment, Suzanne. "Attacking Hillary's Views is Progress." *Los Angeles Times*, August 23, 1992.

Germond, Jack and Jules Witcover. *Mad As Hell: Revolt at the Ballot Box, 1992.* New York: Warner Books, 1993.

Gertzog, Irwin N. *Congressional Women: Their Recruitment, Integration, and Behavior,* 2nd edition. Westport, Conn.: Preager Publishers, 1995.

Gienapp, William E. "Politics Seem to Enter Into Everything." In *Essays on American Antebellum Politics, 1840–1860,* edited by Stephen Maizlish and John Kushma, University of Texas Press, 1982.

Goldman, Peter, Thomas M. DeFrank, Mark Miller, Andrew Murr, Tom Mathews. *Quest for the Presidency: 1992.* College Station: Texas A & M University Press, 1994.

Goldstein, Steve. "Role Unclear for Mrs. Dole." *The News and Observer,* July 24, 1996: A4.

Goodwin, Doris Kearns. *No Ordinary Time: Franklin and Eleanor Roosevelt: The Home Front in World War II.* New York: Simon and Schuster, 1994.

Goodwin, Doris Kearns. "Hillary & Eleanor." *Mother Jones,* January/February, 1993.

Goodwin, Doris Kearns. "For Roosevelt Biographer, Clinton Role Is Unwritten." *Washington Post,* November 24, 1994: B20.

Gould, Lewis. "Modern First Ladies in Historical Perspective." *Presidential Studies Quarterly* 15, 1985: 532–540.

Gould, Lewis. *American First Ladies: Their Lives and Their Legacy.* New York: Garland Publishing, 1996.

Grace, Stephanie. "Mrs. Dole in N.O. to Close Gender Gap; 300 GOP Women Show Support." *The Times-Pacayune*, July 14, 1996: B1.

Greenfield, Meg. "Mrs. President." *Newsweek*. June 20, 1977: 100.

Greenfield, Meg. "Did She Take the Hill?" *Newsweek*, October 11, 1993: 72.

Greer, Germaine. "Abolish Her." *The New Republic*, June 26, 1995: 21–27.

Grimes, Ann. *Running Mates*. New York: Morrow, 1990.

Gutin, Myra. *The President's Partner: The First Lady in the Twentieth Century*. Westport, Conn.: Greenwood Press, 1989.

Guy, Mary. "Hillary, Health Care, and Gender Power." In *Gender Power, Leadership and Governance*, Eds. Georgia Duerst-Lahti and Rita Mae Kelly. Ann Arbor: University of Michigan Press, 1995.

Hall, Mimi. "Hillary Clinton: Asset or Liability?" *USA TODAY*, July 10, 1992: 1.

Harden, Blaine. "Finely Tailored Roles; Candidates' Wives Display Distinct Campaign Styles." *Washington Post,* October 1, 1996: A1.

Hart, Betsy. "How Should First Lady Be Judged?" *Rocky Mountain News*, October 20, 1994: 56A.

Hart, John. *The Presidential Branch*. New York: Pergamon Press, 1987.

Hartford Courant. "Hillary Clinton Goes to Work." January 24,1993: C2.

Heclo, Hugh, and Lester Salamon. *The Illusion of Presidential Government*. Boulder, Colo.: Westview Press, 1981.

Hoff, Joan. "Hillary Clinton Is No Eleanor Roosevelt." *New York Times*, January 22, 1996.

Hohler, Bob. "Mrs. Clinton vs. Mrs. Dole; Spouses Stump in Clash of Villages and Messages." Boston Globe October 28, 1996: A1.

Hoyt, Mary Finch. "Wives Are Running Mates Too." *The Tampa Tribune,* September 29, 1996: 6.

Hunt, Terence. "First Lady Still Defining Her Role." Associated Press, September 9, 1995.

Ifill, Gwen. "G.O.P. Makes Hillary Clinton Issue of the Day." *New York Times*, August 13, 1992a: A11.

Ifill, Gwen. "Clinton Wants Wife at Cabinet Table." *New York Times*, December 12, 1992.

Ifill, Gwen. "Role in Health Expands Hillary Clinton's Power." *The New York Times,* September 22, 1993.

Jamieson, Kathleen Hall. *Eloquence in an Electronic Age*. New York: Oxford University Press, 1988.

Jamieson, Kathleen Hall. *Beyond the Double Bind*. New York: Oxford University Press, 1995.

Jensen, Faye Lind. "As Awesome Responsibility: Rosalynn Carter as First Lady." *Presidential Studies Quarterly*. 769–775, 1990.

Jensen, Holger. "Hillary Rodham Clinton's Visit to Central Asia—where even her husband hasn't been—is not, we are told, a sightseeing trip." *Denver Rocky Mountain News,* November, 1997: 50A.

Johnson, Haynes and David Broder. *The System.* Boston: Little, Brown, 1996.

Johnston, David. "Memo Places Hillary Clinton at Core of Travel Office Case." *New York Times,* January 1, 1996.

Kahn, Joseph. "As Her Husband's Campaign Struggles, She Hits the Hustings in New Hampshire." *Boston Globe,* February 13, 1992.

Kellerman, Barbara. *All the President's Kin.* New York: The Free Press, 1981.

Kellman, Laurie. "Mrs. Clinton Heads to Former U.S.S.R to Strengthen Economic Ties." Associated Press, November 9, 1997a.

Kellman, Laurie. "Mrs. Clinton Promotes Partnerships with Ex-Soviet Republics." Associated Press, November 11, 1997b.

Kenny, Sally J. "New Research on Gendered Political Institutions." *Political Science Quarterly* 49, 1995: 445–466.

Kerber, Linda. *Women of the Republic: Intellect and Ideology in Revolutionary America.* Chapel Hill: University of North Carolina Press, 1980.

Kerber, Linda. "A Constitutional Right to Be Treated Like American Ladies: Women and the Obligation of Citizenship." In *U.S. History as Women's History,* ed. Linda Kerber, Alice Kessler-Harris, and Kathryn Kish Sklar. Chapel Hill: University of North Carolina Press, 1995.

Kolbert, Elizabeth. "Test Marketing a President." *New York Times Magazine,* August 30, 1992.

Kraditor, Aileen. *The Ideas of the Women's Suffrage Movement.* New York: W.W. Norton, 1965.

La Ganga, Maria. "The Elizabeth Quotient." *Los Angeles Times,* August 7, 1996: E1.

Lehigh, Scott. "A Job Whose Time Is Past." *Boston Globe* January 14, 1996: 61.

Lerner, Gerda. *The Creation of Feminist Consciousness.* New York: Oxford University Press, 1993.

Lewin, Tamar. " A Feminism That Speaks for Itself." *New York Times,* October 3, 1993: A1.

Lewis, Anthony. "Merchants of Hate." *New York Times,* August 21, 1992.

McBee, Susanna. "'Substantive' Talks Are Slated for Mrs. Carter on Latin Trip." *Washington Post,* May 25, 1977.

McBee, Susanna. "Mrs. Carter's Trip Carefully Crafted to Make Policy Points." *Washington Post,* May 29, 1977.

McCarthy, Abigail. "They Just Don't Get It." *Commonweal.* October: 9–10, 1992.

McCarthy, Sheryl. "For Hillary, Cookie Days Are Over." *Newsday,* January, 25: 13, 1993.

McClung, Lori. "First Lady Rates High in Ohio." *Cincinnati Post,* June 7, 1993.

McQuillan, Laurence. "Hillary Clinton Defends U.S. Foreign Aid." Reuters, September 8, 1995.

McRoberts, Flynn and Jerry Thomas. "Hillary Clinton May Be Candidate's Top Asset." *Chicago Tribune,* January 31, 1992: 10.

Mannies, Jo. "Hillary Clinton, Elizabeth Dole Reach Standoff in Public Support." *St. Louis Post-Dispatch,* July 14, 1996: A9.

Malone, Julia. "Hillary Clinton Is Pressured to Rethink Her Role." *Austin American-Statesman,* November 30, 1994.

Mann, Judy. "Hillary Horton?" *The Washington Post,* August 21, 1992.

Marelius, John. "Clinton's Rating Sags: Californians Evenly Split on His Re-election." *San Diego Union Tribune* September 21, 1994: A6.

Mayo, Edith. "The Influence and Power of First Ladies." *Chronicle of Higher Education.* 40 (September 15, 1993): A52.

Mayo, Edith, and Denise Meringolo. *First Ladies: Political Role and Public Image.* Washington, D.C.: Smithsonian Institution, 1994.

Means, Marianne. "Hillary Dons New Personal For Campaign Role." *Dayton Daily News,* September 29, 1996: 11B.

Miami Herald. "First Lady's First Job Is Vital." January 24: M, 1993.

Moore, David, and Lydia Saad. "Hillary Clinton Maintains Public Support." *The Gallup Poll Monthly.* April, 1994: 1517.

Morganthau, Tom. "The President's Partner." *Newsweek,* November 5, 1979: 36–47.

Morrison, Patt. "Time for a Feminist as First Lady?" *Los Angeles Times,* July 14, 1992.

Mughan, Anthony, and Barry C. Burden. "The Candidates' Wives." In *Democracy's Feast,* ed. Herbert Weisberg. Chatham, N.J.: Chatham House Publishers, Inc., 1995.

Mughan, Anthony, and Barry C. Burden. "Hillary Clinton and the President's Reelection." Paper presented at the Annual Meeting of the American Political Science Association, Washington, D.C., 1997.

Muir, Janette Kenner and Lisa M. Benitez. "Redefining the Role of the First Lady: The Rhetorical Style of Hillary Rodham Clinton." In *The Clinton Presidency: Images, Isues, and Communication Strategies,* ed. Robert Denton, Jr. and Rachel Holloway. Westport, Conn.: Preager, 1996.

NaGourney., Adam. "First Lady Assails Votes by D'Amato." *The New York Times,* September 24, 1998: A1.

Neal, Stephen. "Hillary Clinton Ridicule Strikes a Sour Note." *Chicago Sun-Times,* January 31, 1992.

Newsweek. "No Road Show." July 29, 1996:7.

New York Times. "Rosalynn Carter Elected." June 8, 1977: A.

New York Times. "Enemies Lists." October 23, 1994: 18.

Norton, Mary Beth. *Liberty's Daughters.* Boston: Little, Brown and Company, 1980.

O'Connor, Karen and Larry J. Sabato. *American Government: Roots and Reform.* New York: Macmillan Publishing, 1993.

Okin, Susan. *Women in Western Political Thought.* Princeton, N.J.: Princeton University Press, 1979.

Page, Susan. "First Lady: Behind the Numbers." *USA TODAY,* January 26, 1996: A4.

Pear, Robert. "Hillary Clinton Gets Policy Job and New Office." *The New York Times,* January 22, 1993.

Perry, James M. and Jeffrey H. Birnbaum. "'We' the President: Hillary Clinton Turns the First Lady Role Into a Powerful Post." *Wall Street Journal,* January 28, 1993.

Pertman, Adam. "Campaign Spotlight Shines on Hillary Clinton." *Boston Globe,* September 26, 1998: 1.

Pfiffner, James P. *The Modern Presidency.* New York: St Martin's Press, 1994.

Phillips, Anne. *Engendering Democracy.* University Park: The Pennsylvania State University Press, 1991.

Phillips, Ian. "First Lady Decries Sexual Violence, Meets Grandmothers of 'Disappeared.'" Associated Press, October 16, 1997.

Pogrebin, Letty Cottin. "Give Hillary a Break." *The New York Times,* June 8, 1992.

Pollit, Katha. "Are We Ready for a First Lady as First Partner?" *Glamour,* September, 1992.

Pollit, Katha. "The Male Media's Hillary Problem." *The Nation,* May 17, 1993: 657–660.

The Public Perspective. "Hillary Rodham Clinton," July/August: 97, 1993.

Pugh, Clifford. '96 Campaign: Elizabeth Dole: asset and ally; despite problems of her husband's campaign, she's a hit." *Houston Chronicle* October 29, 1996: 4.

Quindlen, Anna. "Public & Private: The Cost of Free Speech." *The New York Times,* February 9, 1994a.

Quindlen, Anna. "Public & Private." *New York Times,* May 7, 1994b.

Quindlen, Anna. "Time Right for Hillary to Alter Image." *Wisconsin State Journal,* October 16, 1994c.

Radcliffe, Donnie. "Hillary Clinton and the Laws of the Campaign." *The Washington Post,* October 30, 1992.

Raum, Tom. "Hillary Image Gets Makeover to Warm, Fuzzy." *The Capital Times*, November 29, 1995: 1.

Reed, Judith. "The First Lady." *Vogue,* 183 December, 1993: 228–33.

Reuters. "Hillary Clinton Announces Aid for Mongolia." September 7, 1995.

Roberts, Roxanne. Hillary Clinton Gets Personal." *Redbook*, March, 1993.

Roberts, Troy. "Hillary Rodham Clinton's Tour of Latin America Embroiled in Controversy." *CBS Morning News.* October 16, 1995.

Robertson, Nan. "Mrs. Nixon Starts 8-Day Trip to Africa." *New York Times.* January 2, 1972.

Rosebush, James. *First Lady, Public Wife.* Lanham, Md.: Madison Books, 1987.

Rosenblatt, Robert, and Edwin Chen. "Clinton Seeks First Lady's Help on New Health Plan." *The Los Angeles Times,* January 22, 1993.

Rosenfeld, Stephen. "Hillary Clinton and the Great Game." *Washington Post*, November 14 1997: A27,.

Rosenthal, A.M. "The First Ladyship." *New York Times*, March 11, 1994.

Ross, Sonya. "Mrs. Clinton Lauds Nicaraguan Strides Toward Democracy." Associated Press, October 13, 1995.

Ryden, Patricia. "A Feminist Analysis of the Constructed Role of First Lady: Hillary Rodham Clinton as First Citizen." Paper presented at the Speech Communication Association Annual Meeting, New Orleans, 1993.

Sacremento Bee. "First Lady Urges Better Care." *Sacramento Bee*, December 4, 1996: A18.

Safire, William. "Blizzard of Lies." *New York Times*, January 8, 1996.

Sapiro, Virginia. *The Political Integration of Women.* Urbana: The University of Illinois Press, 1983.

Sapiro, Virginia and Pamela Conover. "Gender in the 1992 Electorate." Unpublished paper, 1993.

Sheehy, Gail. "What Hillary Wants." *Vanity Fair*, May: 142–47, 212–17, 1992.

Shepard, Alicia C. "The Second Time Around." *American Journalism Review,* June: 29–34, 1994.

Shepard, Paul. "Hillary Clinton Gets a Post-Convention Bounce." *The Record*, September 1, 1996: A24.

Sherrill, Martha. "A Clinton In the Cabinet?" *Washington Post.* December 19, 1992.

Sims, Anastatia. "Beyond the Ballot: The Radical Vision of the Antisuffragists." In *Votes for Women*, ed. Marjorie Spruill Wheeler. Knoxville: University of Tennessee Press, 1995.

Stark, Steven. "Gap Politics." *The Atlantic Monthly*, July: 71–80, 1996.

Stuckey, Mary. "Hillary Clinton as a Cultural Icon." Roundtable paper presented at the annual meeting of the Southern Political Science Association, Savannah, Georgia, 1993.

Tang, Terry. "Fearless First Lady Give Chinese, Critics an Earful." *The Seattle Times*, September 8, 1995: B6.

Tenpas, Kathleen. "Women on the White House Staff: A Longitudinal Analysis (1939–1994)." In *The Other Elites: Women, Politics, and Power in the Executive Branch,* ed. Janet Martin and Maryanne Borrelli. New York: Lynne Reiner, 1997.

Thomas, Helen. "Commentary." United Press International, May 15, 1996.

Thomma, Steven. "First Lady Flourishes in Newfound Role of Nation's Hottest Politician." Knight-Ridder Newspapers as carried in *The Buffalo News,* October 29, 1998: 5A.

Thompson, Joan Hulse. "The Family and Medical Leave Act: A Policy for Families." In *Women in Politics: Outsiders or Insiders?"* ed. Lois Duke Whitaker. Upper Saddle River, N.J.: Prentice Hall, 1999.

Tien, Charles, Regan Checchio, and Arthur H. Miller. "The Impact of Wives on Presidential Campaigns." In *Women in Politics: Outsiders or Insiders?"* 3rd edition, ed. Lois Duke Whitaker. Upper Saddle River, N.J.: Prentice Hall, 1999.

Time. "African Queen for a Week." January 17, 1972: 12–14.

Toner, Robin. "Backlash for Hillary Clinton Puts Negative Image to Rout." *New York Times*, September 24, 1992.

Troy, Gil. *Affairs of State.* New York: The Free Press, 1996.

Tyler, Patrick E. "Hillary Clinton in China Details Abuse of Women." *New York Times*, September 6, 1995: A1.

U.S. News and World Report. "Rosalynn's Turn at Diplomacy 'Family Style.'" June 6, 1977: 36.

Walsh, Kenneth. "Now the First Chief Advocate," *U.S. News & World Report*, January 25, 1993: 46–50.

Walsh, Kenneth, Matthew Cooper, and Gloria Borger. "Taking Their Measure." *U.S. News & World Report*, January 31, 1994: 42–48.

Walsh, Kenneth. "Hillary's Resurrection." *U.S. News & World Report*, October 20, 1997: 26.

Wieck, Paul. "GOP Should Substitute Elizabeth Dole for Husband Bob." *Albuquerque Journal*, July 24, 1996: A10.

Wills, Gary. "H.R. Clinton's Case." *New York Review of Books*, 39, 1992: 3–5.

Woodward, Bob. *The Agenda: Inside the Clinton White House.* New York: Simon & Schuster, 1994.

Wooten, Jim. "Hillary Clinton, Tammy Wynette: Both are Winners." *The Atlanta Journal and Constitution*, February 2, 1992.

Zabarenko, Deborah. "Stand by Your Man? New Look in Campaign Wives." Reuters. February 4, 1992.

Index